Beginning With Jesus

Christ in Scripture,
the Church,
and Discipleship

Joel B. Green

Beginning With Jesus

ISBN 0-687-05713-2

00 01 02 03 04 05 06 07 08 09—10 9 8 7 6 5 4 3 2 1
Manufactured in the United States of America.

Contents

1

Christology: The Journey

Key Concepts:
- What is "Christology"?
- What is the relationship between understanding who Jesus is and following him in faithful discipleship?
- How is Jesus related to the Old and New Testaments?
- What is the role of the creeds and of doctrine in helping us to understand the nature and work of Jesus Christ and in shaping the church's identity?

Why should we Christians be concerned with "Christology," that is, with how we understand the nature and work of Jesus Christ? An immediate and provocative answer to this question is provided by the name *Christian* itself.

According to Acts 11:26, "it was in Antioch that the disciples were first called 'Christians.'" Notice that they were first called Christians; they did not first refer to themselves in this way. Originally, the term was one of scorn and ridicule, coined by those who were hostile to followers of Jesus. From early on, "Christians" were regarded as Christ-minions, hangers-on to a man who had been executed as a common criminal. The term appears as well in 1 Peter 4:16, with regard to people who had so identified with Jesus that their allegiance to him was expressed in their humiliation and suffering "as Christians."

5

The name we share, *Christian*, ties us to Christ—not to an idea or to a precept, but to a person from Nazareth whose life marks for us the turning of the ages. To speak of Christ is at the same time to speak of our own lives, and to speak of authentic human life is to refer to him.

It has always been so. When in Mark's Gospel, Jesus asks of his followers, "Who do you say that I am?" (8:29), he is not bringing to conclusion a Bible trivia contest or playing an ancient form of the game show "Jeopardy." He is not testing the knowledge his disciples have amassed. Rather, he is engaged in what will become before the story is finished a life-and-death struggle to communicate faithfully his messianic mission. He asks this question because who we understand Jesus to be is intimately tied to what response we make to him and his message.

From earliest times, then, Christology involved people in far more than flights of speculation. "Who do you say that I am?" is not a polite conversation starter. Here we have to do with the very ground of our life, but not only our life. Here we have to do with what it means to be vitally human, to live a life that grasps fully the existence set before us by the gracious God who created all of life. Christology ties together our deepest beliefs about God; our loftiest hopes about humanity; and, indeed, our greatest concerns about the universe in which we live.

In this chapter I want to introduce the content of Christology by borrowing the image of the journey. This metaphor is especially useful because faithful life before God is often depicted as a journey or pilgrimage, because our understanding of the person and work of Jesus involves exploring his significance, and because our own progress in the adventure of discipleship is pivotal to our coming to know about Jesus fully.

The Journey of Jesus

Christology is a journey—actually it entails three journeys on which we embark all at once. There is first the journey of Jesus recorded in the four Gospels of the New Testament. Looking over the shoulders of those women and men who followed him, even joining with them in the

Gospel narratives, we explore the manner of his life. We see him at prayer, nurturing his relationship with God and aligning his own life purpose with the will of God. We see him at table with Israelites of all kinds—women and toll agents, sinners and Pharisees—expounding on the ways of God and opening to all persons the experience of God's goodness. We see him reading the Scriptures of Israel, which we know as the Old Testament, reading his life in light of the ongoing story of God's relationship to Israel.

This reminds us that we cannot follow the journey of Jesus as though it began with Jesus' birth sometime between 6–4 B.C. Jesus was a Jew, and the fundamental categories by which he would have communicated and by which his own contemporaries would have understood him were deeply rooted in Israel's own walk with God. Thus, the story of Jesus draws its meaning from the ancient and high drama of God's promises to Abraham; God's liberation of Israel from slavery in Egypt under the leadership of Moses; God's interventions on behalf of Sarah and Hannah; and God's pledge to David, king of Israel, that his dynasty over the people of God would be everlasting. As the ancestral list provided in Matthew's opening chapter declares, the story of Jesus is intertwined with the theater and suspense of Rahab and Ruth, Hezekiah and Manasseh, and others of Israel's past (Matthew 1:1-17). Here, then, is a key affirmation: We cannot know Jesus Christ genuinely apart from the God of Jesus Christ revealed first in the Scriptures of Israel. The Christ proclaimed in the New Testament cannot be grasped apart from an understanding of the God who raised Jesus from the dead, and this God is the one who revealed himself in many and various ways within ancient Israel. The Old Testament is thus more than a preface to the good news of Jesus Christ. It is the revelatory narrative of God's dealings with Israel, the story of God's saving purpose that culminates in the advent of Jesus. The Old Testament prepares the way of the Lord, and the New Testament proclaims that the Word became flesh and dwelt among us.

The first journey is exploratory, an excursion that meanders through the life of Israel; that surveys the routes of Israel's longings, its expectations for restoration; and that

1,

"Jesus was a Jew." This truism is not often contemplated by Christians today. Why do you suppose this is the case? How would our understanding and practices be shaped if we took Jesus' roots in the people of Israel more seriously?

reaches its destination in Jesus' messianic pilgrimage throughout Galilee and up to Jerusalem where he fulfilled Israel's hopes and God's ancient purpose.

The Journey About Jesus

The second journey comprises an expedition begun already in Jesus' own lifetime, one that continues to this very day. Here we probe Jesus' significance. Begun in fits and starts by his own followers, the trek continued under the guidance of writers like Luke, John, and Paul, who expounded on the meaning of Jesus' mission for varied audiences throughout the Roman Empire. The journey continues beyond the pages of the New Testament, through the great controversies of the early church, through the age of reformation in the sixteenth century, to our own day. Knowing Jesus genuinely is inseparable from the church's ongoing struggle to grasp the importance of Jesus for faith and life.

Participating in this second journey reminds us that the significance of Jesus was not fully transparent to his mother as she held him as a newborn in her arms. Who Jesus was and is, his nature and identity, were not clear to his first disciples either. Throughout the history of the church, across the globe, even today, we recognize that believers like us have continued to find fresh meaning for our lives in the coming of Jesus. How do we get from the apparent simplicity of a manger scene in ancient Bethlehem to our most profound hymns and confessional statements about Jesus?

The trail head of this expedition, this second journey, is the New Testament itself, since it is here that we find some of our earliest reflection on the importance of Jesus in God's purpose. Seen in this way, Jesus is the center of Scripture. The Old Testament looks forward to the advent of Jesus Christ, and it is against the horizons of Israel's faith that Jesus carried on his work. The New Testament takes Jesus Christ as its starting point and looks back upon him as the measure of faithfulness and the ultimate disclosure of God's fidelity and goodness toward his people.

The New Testament as Witness to Christ

Within the New Testament, the four Gospels are consumed above all with Jesus' adult life and the contours of his mission. Like a magnificently woven sweater, they portray the significance of Jesus by cross-weaving the warp of his words and deeds with the woof of God's plan witnessed in the Scriptures. Jesus is like the great deliverer and prophet Moses, but he is more. He reminds us of Elijah and Elisha, but their lives do scarcely more than point to the importance of his. He is the righteous one who suffers unjustly, the servant whose suffering brings redemption, and more.

The Acts of the Apostles shifts the focus of the story to the activity of the Holy Spirit and of faithful witnesses who carry on the work of Jesus following his departure. Jesus is not absent, however. After all, according to Acts, it is none other than Jesus who pours out the Holy Spirit on God's people; and it is in the name of Jesus that people are baptized and by that name that people are healed. Jesus may be dead, but he is risen. Jesus may be ascended into the heavens; but he is present, through the Spirit and through his followers, to bring salvation.

The New Testament letters tell little of the life of Jesus, but they are nonetheless concerned with its enduring gravity. Whether addressed to a specific house church (for example, the Letter to Philemon) or to the churches in a larger geographical region (for example, Second Corinthians), these documents articulate in changing times and places the tenacious relevance of Jesus. Preaching at the home of Cornelius, Peter had proclaimed that Jesus is "Lord of all" (Acts 10:36); and the New Testament letters spell out this cosmic, universal affirmation in particular, down-to-earth circumstances.

The New Testament's last book, Revelation, looks backward on the coming of Jesus but also looks forward upon the consummation of God's purpose at the end time. Life in the present must be lived in light of the future; and Revelation portrays that future as belonging to and determined by Jesus, the Lamb of God.

From "Rule of Faith" to "Ecumenical Creed"

The New Testament provides authoritative witness to Jesus Christ, but it does not answer all the questions that might be posed about him. In fact, sometimes the New Testament seems to raise more questions than it answers. If Jesus is the fulfillment of Israel's hopes, why did Israel as a whole not welcome him as God's envoy of salvation? If, as Jews and Christians believe, God is one and there is only one God, why do we find believers praying to Jesus as though he were God? In addition, the New Testament does not always answer similar questions in similar ways. Influenced by different traditions of thought and addressing a variety of exigencies, New Testament writers present a sometimes dizzying array of titles and images for Jesus (Son of Man, Suffering Servant, Son of God, Prophet Like Moses, Son of David, Son of Abraham, Christ/Messiah, Lord, Lamb, Pioneer, Savior, Living Stone, and more). What is more, the nature of the New Testament witness to Jesus itself provides a model for further exploration of Jesus' significance in fresh and unfolding circumstances. Just as Jesus' message for Galilean peasants had to be recast by Paul for Roman urbanites, so the spread of the good news would require further insight into the meaning of Jesus for new settings and problems.

In the years marking the close of the period of the first apostles and in subsequent decades, Christian literature was to become more and more explicit in its understanding of Jesus' identity. As we will see, we find definite but infrequent evidence of Jesus' deity or pre-existence in the pages of the New Testament; but even these references stand in contrast to the matter-of-fact statements we find in the second century. For example, Ignatius, the early second-century bishop of Antioch in Syria, referred to Jesus as "Jesus Christ our God"[1] and even puzzled over the paradox of the Incarnation: How could Jesus be both human and God, flesh and spirit?

Related to questions of this more philosophical nature is the variety of interpretations of Jesus' nature and identity—

and, indeed, the nature of Christian faith—that began to arise in the second century. Simply put, the New Testament, with its many writers and concerns, does not speak with a monotone. In its pages we hear more of a choir than a solo, with different writers giving more or less prominence to different aspects of Jesus' person and work. By giving one New Testament voice primacy over another (and so on), it has always been possible to depict Jesus, using texts from the same books, in contradictory ways. The Gospels and Letters did not come with manuals that would ensure proper usage or predetermined conclusions. Tertullian (*ca.* A.D. 160–*ca.* 230), the first great Latin Christian writer of Christian material, rightly saw that the advent of Jesus was and is not self-interpreting and that some manner for arbitrating significant differences of viewpoint is required. How could the early church determine which portrait of Jesus was more faithful to God's eternal purpose? Among the many possible, competing attempts to portray Jesus' significance, which were authentic?

As Tertullian developed his thinking on this matter, he was joined by others beginning in the mid-second century A.D.—including Irenaeus, Clement of Alexandria, Hippolytus, Origen, and Novatian—in appealing to a "Rule of Faith" or "Rule of Truth" in order to determine the soundness of biblical interpretations and theological formulations. Precursors to the later, more formal creeds of the ecumenical church, these "rules" summarized the heart of Christian faith and served as theological boundary markers for Christian identity. Thus, for example, Tertullian wrote,

> Now with regard to this rule of faith . . . it is, you must know, that which prescribes the belief that there is only one God, and that he is none other than the creator of the world, who produced all things out of nothing through his own word, first of all sent forth. This word is called his son, and, under the name of God, was seen in diverse manners by the patriarchs, heard at all times in the prophets, and at last brought by the Spirit and

power of the Father down into the virgin Mary. He was made flesh in her womb, and, being born of her, went forth as Jesus Christ. Thereafter, he preached the new land and the new promise of the kingdom of heaven, and he worked miracles. Having been crucified, he rose again on the third day. Having ascended into the heavens, he sat at the right hand of the Father. He sent in place of himself the power of the Holy Spirit to lead those who believe. He will come with glory to take the saints to the enjoyment of everlasting life and of the heavenly promises, and to condemn the wicked to everlasting fire. This will take place after the resurrection of both these classes, together with the restoration of their flesh. This rule . . . was taught by Christ, and raises among us no other questions than those which heresies introduce, and which make people heretics.[2]

2.

Early "Rules of Faith" and the great creeds of the church were formulated in climates of controversy, where the identity of the church was at stake. In what ways might the church of the early twenty-first century find its identity in these confessions?

"Rules of Faith" from these early centuries generally possess a narrative quality and confessional tone similar to Tertullian's proposal. By them, the church came to determine its own theological commitments and to confirm (or condemn) on that basis those interpretations that are formative (or not) of Christian faith and practice. Today, these "Rules of Faith" have taken the form of the Apostles' Creed, often recited in services of worship.

Controversy within the church in the second and third centuries thus focused on Christology. Although the construction of "Rules of Faith" addressed the problem, they provided no decisive solution. They carried no authority outside of themselves. Resolution came, rather, through the decisions of the ecumenical councils of the church.

The Council of Nicaea (A.D. 325) found that Jesus was God's Son in the fullest sense of the word; Jesus is "of the same substance with the Father." Although using language not found in Scripture, church leaders gathered in Nicaea believed that, with this language, they were expressing nothing less nor more than the plain teaching of Scripture. Actually dating from later in the fourth century (that is,

Beginning With Jesus

from the Council of Constantinople [A.D. 381]), the Nicene Creed (as represented in *The United Methodist Hymnal* [1989, 880]) affirms,

We believe in one Lord, Jesus Christ,
    the only Son of God,
    eternally begotten of the Father;
    God from God, Light from Light,
    true God from true God;
    begotten, not made,
    of one Being with the Father;
    through him all things were made.

The creed goes on to emphasize Jesus' humanity:

[Who] was incarnate of the Holy Spirit and the
Virgin Mary, and became truly human.

Accordingly, Jesus was "very God" and "very human," "truly God" and "truly human."

How can Jesus be both God and human? This question was taken up in the next century, at the Council of Chalcedon (A.D. 451):

In agreement, therefore, with the holy fathers we all unanimously teach that we should confess one and the same Christ, Son, Lord, only-begotten, made known in two natures without confusion, without change, without division, without separation, the difference of the natures being by no means removed because of the union but the property of each nature being preserved and coalescing in one person and one substance, not parted or divided into two persons but one and the same Son, only-begotten, divine Word, the Lord Jesus Christ.[3]

That is, at Chalcedon the church answered the question of Jesus' nature by speaking of one person and two natures, divine and human. It is important to notice that this statement is largely negative ("without," "in no wise," "not as if"), suggesting that it has always been easier to say what is not the case than to say what is. Even such negative statements have a crucial role to play, however; for they specify the boundaries within which the church operates.

Christology and Christian Witness

These old struggles over Christology may seem to some today to be much ado about very little, as little more than mental gymnastics or theological swashbuckling. For others Christological discussion is a power play. Who can put forward the best argument? Whose side will win? Who gets to define Christian faith for the rest of us? Undoubtedly, discussion regarding the nature and work of Christ has been carried on from all sorts of motivations, some easier to justify than others. Concerns of this nature must not distract us from the central reality that, in such discussion, the stakes are high indeed. Christology is not an add-on to our faith, as though it were interesting but dispensable.

Consider the witness of Basil of Caesarea (*ca.* A.D. 329–379), for example. One of the main champions of Nicene faith, Basil regarded the affirmation of Christ's deity (as well as that of the Holy Spirit) as essential for the church's witness in the world and ministry among society's poor. One of the heresies against which he fought, known as Arianism, insisted that the Son was subordinate to the Father—a view that led in practical terms to a hierarchical account of all of creation, with all creatures, including the Son, assigned to different levels of importance. In this case, theology and social politics ran hand-in-hand, with Arianism providing a ready source of legitimacy for the plight of the poor and the supreme imperial power of the Roman emperor.

Basil perceived God as a divine community: one substance, three persons, with the Son and the Spirit not subordinate to God, but themselves divine. This view worked itself out in Basil's world as a model for human community where all are regarded as having the same footing. Accordingly, the wealthy have no inbred primacy; the poor are not inherently less important; and people are not destined for this or that social class. Armed with this full-bodied Trinitarian theology, Basil was able to articulate a prophetic word over against the dehumanizing practices of the wealthy and those of the higher social classes, in favor of the common good. Is it any wonder, then, that Basil was threatened by the state, by the social elite, and by the wealthy of his day? Christology matters!

The Creeds and the Church

Throughout its history, the church has almost universally affirmed and supported the Christological statements that grew out of the ecumenical councils. This is true of the Eastern and Western churches and of the churches of the Reformation, so that all three major branches of the church (Orthodox, Roman Catholic, and Protestant) have embraced the ancient creeds. This includes, of course, John Wesley, himself an Anglican, and the churches that trace their heritage through him. Article II of The Articles of Religion of The Methodist Church resonates with the language of Nicaea and Chalcedon:

> The Son, who is the Word of the Father, the very and eternal God, of one substance with the Father, took man's nature in the womb of the blessed Virgin; so that two whole and perfect natures, that is to say, the Godhead and Manhood, were joined together in one person, never to be divided; whereof is one Christ, very God and very Man.[4]

In his own writings, Wesley uses the creeds almost as a second language, using phrases like "real God as real man"[5] and speaking of the two natures of Jesus, divine and human. In his "Letter to a Roman Catholic," he wrote of Jesus, "He is the proper, natural Son of God, God of God, very God of very God."[6] Reflecting on Acts 10:36 in his *Explanatory Notes on the New Testament*, Wesley names Jesus "the God-man."[7]

The United Methodist tradition is not unique in its affirmation of the Christological formulations of the ecumenical councils but on this matter is one with other traditions of the Protestant Reformation. With the dawn of the Enlightenment, and with it the Modern Era, the central Christological beliefs of the church have been called into question.

That questions should arise in the Age of Enlightenment should not surprise us, since "history," including historic beliefs, has always been troublesome in the modern period. As with "modern" architecture or "modern" science, "modern" theology has been characterized by its indifference to history, by its attempt to define itself not so much *against* the past, as *detached* from it. We whose lives grew out of the Enlightenment have tended to experience the past as a burden, as intellectual handcuffs that inhibit freedom and stifle creativity. For "modern" people, the hero does not stand on the accomplishments of others but is self-made. The ancient creeds have no particular relevance for us, according to this way of thinking, since they belong to another people in another time. We must be completely unhindered to construct our own beliefs. These ways of thinking have played havoc with our understanding of and ability to embrace the great creeds of the church. For this reason, some prophets within the church today speak of our theological amnesia and worry aloud about our theological illiteracy.

Some say that we live in the time of "Late Modernity"; others say that we have already entered into a "Postmodern" age. However one wants to classify the era in which we live, it is nonetheless true that, today, we are learning to think not so much "in the absence of history," as "with history." For Christians, this is a vital recognition. This is true, first, because what it means to "be Christian" is inseparably linked with past events. Christian faith, like the Jewish faith out of which it grew, is fundamentally defined by the belief that God reveals his purpose *in history*. For Christians, God's nature and purpose are revealed definitively in a particular history, the historical figure of Jesus of Nazareth. Second, we are not the first people to read Scripture, nor will we be the last. Nor are we the first (or last) to contemplate the significance of the coming of Jesus. In fact, key to our faith is our identity with the people of God in times past and future. The people of God in Jesus' day, the people of God at the end time—they are we; we are that people. Their faith is ours and ours theirs. To use the image of Hebrews 11, they join us in the coliseum as a great crowd of witnesses, urging us on in the faith, just as we, once we have joined that crowd, will urge others on as well.

We will say more about these challenges in the pages that follow. For now, it is enough to have embarked this far on our exploration of how the historic church has understood the significance of Jesus. On this journey, we can be assured that the terrain has already been mapped, with sign posts placed along the way.

The Journey With Jesus

The first journey we identified was the journey *of* Jesus, a trek of exploration that took seriously the life of Jesus in ancient Palestine and the significance of Jesus as a Jew whose mission was oriented toward the restoration of the people of God. The second was a journey *about* Jesus, an expedition through New Testament texts and the Christian tradition charged with articulating the importance of Jesus in new times and places. Being Christian is related to both of these; for our faith is grounded in the unique figure of Jesus, his life and his message. In turn, his significance is drawn from the ancient story of God's purpose on display in Israel's Scriptures and in Israel's hopes; and his impress is seen on every page of the New Testament and, more or less clearly, throughout the history of the church.

There is a third journey, which I have called the journey *with* Jesus. The first assumes that, without the historical person Jesus, there is no Christology. The second assumes that the subject of Christology cannot be limited to the historical person who was crucified under Pontius Pilate in A.D. 30 or 33. The third journey begins with the admission that knowing Jesus entails far more than knowing or even confessing aloud the church's Christological beliefs. **Christology is also learning to know Jesus in the life of dis-**

3,

Think about your own spiritual journey. What were your earliest conceptions of Jesus? In what ways have your perceptions changed over time?

cipleship. The two, theories and beliefs about Jesus' significance and the faith and practices that distinguish Christian life, are really not two but one. When Jesus asked the question, "Who do you say that I am?" he knew he was asking two questions at once. This is because the two are inseparably intertwined, beliefs about and belief in Christ. Knowing that Jesus is Lord *and* doing the word of the Lord—this is where knowing Jesus as Lord is fully realized.

This emphasis comes to the fore in a way that is often overlooked in Mark's account of the appointing of the twelve apostles. Earlier (for example, Mark 1:16-20), Jesus had invited persons to join him in his mission. In Mark 3:13-19, he appoints them to that mission; they are to cast their lots with him and are designated to preach and to engage in battle against evil forces just as he does. Notice, however, the two prongs of their appointment: "Jesus went up the mountain and called to him those whom he wanted, and they came to him. And he appointed twelve, whom he also named apostles, to be with him, and to be sent out to proclaim the message, and to have authority to cast out demons" (Mark 3:13-15).

We may think of apostleship, or Christian leadership in general, in terms of *doing*; the accent for us may easily fall on deeds of power, communicating the Word of God, and other forms of ministry. In this text, however, the highest priority is given to *being with Jesus.* This "being with Jesus" is not spelled out in the Gospel of Mark in mystical ways; these apostles join Jesus on his way, walk with him, eat with him, listen to him, and share with him both when he is extended hospitality by others and when he is rejected. All of life (and with it, all forms of knowing) is constructed around this relationship. Being with Jesus, not performing great things for him, is their primary call. There is no "sending" without this "being with." Only as people are free toward God through their companionship with Jesus are they genuinely free toward the neighbor who needs them. The journey of Christology, the journey *with* Jesus, is thus not aimed simply at embracing and passing on a tradition about the nature and work of Christ; it embraces as well, and fundamentally, our being shaped by communion with him so that we might know Jesus intimately.

4,

Learning about Jesus and learning with Jesus— both are central to our faith. Has one or the other of these emphases been pursued to the neglect of the other in your community of believers? If so, how might this balance be redressed?

The invitation to Christology is an invitation to discipleship, to align oneself with Christ just as Christ aligned his life with the will of God. Christology is realized, then, on Sunday morning in the congregational recitation of the Apostles' Creed; but it is also realized on Monday as the community of Christ is led to serve and to lift up those whose lives are lived on society's periphery. "Proclaim the good news, 'The kingdom of heaven has drawn near,' " Jesus directs those who follow. "Cure the sick, raise the dead, cleanse the lepers, cast out demons. You received without payment; give without payment" (Matthew 10:7-8). Learning about Christ entails learning with Christ. Christology is the journey of discipleship.

[1] Compare, for example, *Epistle to the Ephesians*, 18:2, by Ignatius; *Epistle to the Romans*, 3:3; *Epistle to the Smyrneans*, 1:1; and others.
[2] From *De Praescriptaene Haereticarum*, 13.
[3] From *The Story of Christian Theology: Twenty Centuries of Tradition and Reform*, by Roger E. Olson (InterVarsity, 1999); pages 231–32.
[4] From *The Book of Discipline of The United Methodist Church*, 1996 (Copyright © 1996 The United Methodist Publishing House); page 57.
[5] From *Explanatory Notes Upon the New Testament*, by John Wesley (Epworth, 1976); on Philippians 2:6.
[6] From "Letter to a Roman Catholic," by John Wesley, in *John Wesley*, edited by Albert C. Outler, Library of Christian Thought (Oxford University Press, 1964); page 494.
[7] From *Explanatory Notes Upon the New Testament*, on Acts 10:36.

2
Israel's Hopes, God's Fulfillment

Key Concepts:
- How realistic is it to speak of "what Jews expected" in Jesus' day?
- What Jewish expectations merged in the hope for an ideal king to reestablish the Davidic monarchy?
- How would Jesus' contemporaries have understood the "kingdom of God"?
- What does it mean to say that the Scriptures of Israel are fulfilled in Christ?

The Gospel of Mark opens with the declaration, we might even say the assumption, that Jesus is the Messiah or Christ (Mark 1:1). In Paul's letters, "Christ" seems at times almost to function as Jesus' second name. Based on evidence like this from the New Testament, Christians throughout the last two millennia have grown accustomed to declaring that Jews in Jesus' day were expecting a Messiah and that Jesus was that long-awaited Messiah. In reality, the picture is somewhat more complicated.

The problems we face in this chapter may surprise many Christians. Jewish scholars have long complained that Christians have too often allowed the New Testament to represent for them the sum total of the first-century Jewish world. In recent decades, far more attention has been paid to other literature representing the faith and hopes of Jews in first-century Palestine. This work has been helped along by the discovery and subsequent publication and study of the Dead Sea Scrolls. Although we may wish we knew more than we do about "common Judaism"—that is, the life and beliefs of everyday Jews—we now know far more than we did, say, in the mid-twentieth century. The result is that we have a clearer picture of the variegated nature of Jewish life in Jesus' world and thus a better sense of how Jesus and the movement he spawned might have fit within and added to the larger mural of Judaism in the Roman world. Drawing on this recent study, the agenda in this chapter is to establish the context and content of Israel's messianic hopes.

The Idea of a Messiah in Israel

The term *Christ* is an English transliteration of the Greek word *Christos*, which corresponds to the Hebrew term *māsîaḥ*, or "Messiah." The two words, *Christ* and *Messiah*, refer to an anointed person and are interchangeable. The term itself is used sparsely and with little consistency in the literature of Judaism before the time of Jesus. In fact, talk of "the Jewish expectation of a Messiah" in the decades or even centuries leading up to the birth of Jesus makes so many wrongheaded assumptions that, in the end, we are better off focusing elsewhere.

Many Christians assume that the landscape of the Old Testament is littered with prophecies of the coming Messiah. Actually, the word *Messiah* or *Christ* is never used in the Old Testament of a future ruler or deliverer. The favorite "messianic prophecies" to which Christians have turned typically include no specific mention of the Messiah at all. For example, a key figure in the fourth-century church, Athanasius, Bishop of Alexandria, while proving the messiahship of Jesus, wrote,

> Nor is even his death passed over in silence; on the contrary it is referred to in the divine Scriptures, even exceeding clearly. For to the end that none should err for want of instruction in the actual events, they feared not to mention even the cause

of his death—that he suffers it, not for his own sake, but for the immortality and salvation of all, and the counsels of the Jews against him and the indignities offered him at their hands.[1]

Athanasius went on to support his claims with extended quotations of Isaiah 53:3-10, a prophetic passage portraying the suffering servant of the Lord. Such biblical texts Athanasius regarded as speaking of Jesus "even exceeding clearly."[2] In fact, however, the term *Messiah* is absent from this text and, indeed, from the larger unit in which it is located (Isaiah 52:13–53:12). What is more, in the historical period leading up to the birth of Jesus, Jewish speculation about the Messiah never focused either on this Isaianic text or more generally on the figure of a suffering servant.

"Messiah" does appear in the Old Testament, of course; but there it designates Davidic kings, past and present, as "anointed ones" or "anointed" (for example, 2 Chronicles 6:42; Psalms 18:50; 89:20). "Anointed" is also used of Cyrus in Isaiah 45:1 and of still another king in Habakkuk 3:13. Priests are also called "anointed" (for example, Leviticus 4:5, 16), as are prophets (for example, "anointed ones" in 1 Chronicles 16:22). Clearly, "christ" is not a technical term in the Old Testament for the coming deliverer.

Judaism contemporary with Jesus is often called Second Temple Judaism, since this was the period of the rebuilding and use of the Second Temple (the first having been destroyed in the early sixth century B.C.). In Second Temple Judaism, the term *Messiah* is used infrequently but in potentially promising ways. In the Psalms of Solomon, we read of a future Christ, a king in the lineage of David, who will destroy the unrighteous rulers, purge Jerusalem of Gentiles, drive out sinners, smash the arrogance of sinners, destroy the unlawful nation, condemn sinners, gather a holy people, and judge the tribes. The Dead Sea Scrolls anticipate a royal messiah *and* a priestly messiah, and we find evidence here of a prophetic deliverer as well. Among this body of literature, however, we find no consensus on the nature of the Messiah or on what this figure (or figures) is expected to accomplish.

All in all, though, the evidence is slim, and all the more so if we ask how representative of the whole of Judaism these texts might prove to be. This question is exacerbated further when we remember that Judaism in the first century was a large umbrella, a name for many different forms of Judaism. Hence, when we hear the question, What did first-century Jews expect? our immediate response must always be, Which ones? The most that can be said (and this certainly ought to be said) is that in some strands of first-century Judaism, the hope was nurtured that God would send or raise up a figure who would serve as his envoy of salvation.

The Promise of a Davidic King: A Second Look

It is a long way from the rather meager results of our summary of expectations related to a coming Christ among first-century Jews to the extravagant claims made on Jesus' behalf in the New Testament and subsequently in Christian history. In part, this has to do with how we have asked the question thus far. If we work with larger categories of thought, much more can be said.

According to 2 Samuel 7:12-16, God had promised to David an everlasting dynasty, an expectation that came into full bloom in the life of Jesus, according to Luke. Compare, for example, Nathan's prophetic words to David with the words of Gabriel as he announced the birth of Jesus to Mary:

2 Samuel 7:12-16
I will raise up your offspring after you, who shall come forth from your body, and I will establish *his kingdom*. He shall build a house for my name, and I will *establish the throne of his kingdom forever. I will be a father to him, and he shall be a son to me.* . . . Your house and *your kingdom shall be made sure forever before me; your throne shall be established forever.*

Luke 1:30-35

Do not be afraid, Mary, for you have found favor with God. And now, you will conceive in your womb and bear a son, and you will name him Jesus. He will be great, and will be called the *Son of the Most High*, and the Lord God will give to him *the throne of his ancestor David. He will reign over the house of Jacob forever, and of his kingdom there will be no end.*

Of course, the message of Gabriel translates the expectation of a dynasty ("house"), envisioned in Nathan's prophecy, to a single ruler, Jesus, reigning forever. This is because, in Jesus' ministry, the reign of David has been correlated with the definitive, everlasting kingdom of the Lord God. How do we get from Second Samuel to Luke, particularly when the contingencies of history did not allow for a literal fulfillment of God's promise to David, whose dynasty was interrupted for centuries?

Already in the eighth-century prophets, and especially in Isaiah, we find evidence of a renewed hope for the restoration of Israel as one nation under a new Davidic ruler (see Isaiah 9:1-7; 11:1-5). Although these prophetic texts may borrow ideas from earlier times when a Davidic king did occupy the throne, they nonetheless express hope in a future, ideal king. Isaiah 11:1-5 is especially important in this regard, with its image of a "shoot" from the stump of Jesse and "branch" embraced as a favorite in later expectation (for example, Jeremiah 23:5-6; 33:14-26). The king to come will be a righteous judge who will demonstrate mercy to the oppressed; he will be endowed with the Spirit and possess extraordinary wisdom and virtue. In these and other texts the word *messiah* is missing, but messianic ideas are nonetheless present.

After the fall of Jerusalem in 586 B.C., hopes for Israel's restoration under an ideal, Davidic king waned until they were rekindled in the first century B.C. As we have already noted, the Psalms of Solomon contain a prayer that the Lord raise up a son of David as king to rule over Israel. The Qumran scrolls similarly reflect an interest in a Davidic messiah. Other Jewish texts, First Enoch and Fourth Ezra, witness a recovery of royal-Davidic hope and imagery. In this later period, hope for a Davidic king is still structured around the restoration of Israel; but now the focus expands to include the need for this figure to challenge the false claims of other rulers. Before he can restore Israel, he must deliver the people from other, Gentile overlords.

The tradition of expectation focused on the ideal king to reestablish the Davidic monarchy is thus diverse, but it coalesces around three points:

(1) The coming king will be dependent on and obedient to the Lord God.
(2) The coming king must be instrumental in establishing the Kingdom, which entails driving out or destroying the wicked and gathering the people of God.
(3) This restoration is marked as an end time (or eschatological) event, in which a new era of peace and righteousness is introduced.

What this means is that when we sing songs of expectation of the coming Messiah, we should recognize that our Christian interpretations of the coming of Jesus in the history of the world must not be confused with the realities of Jewish expectation in the decades or centuries before Jesus. In the hymn "O Come, O Come, Emmanuel," we sing,

> O come, O come, Emmanuel,
> and ransom captive Israel,
> that mourns in lonely exile here
> until the Son of God appear.[3]

These words have great meaning on this side of Christmas. We might even imagine that these words speak to the inner longings of all people everywhere. But this is not to say that Jesus fulfilled particularly Jewish expectations. This is true, first, because (we must continually remind ourselves) not all Jews saw things in the same way. Some, not all, Jews expected divine deliverance through a Davidic king. Second, we must realize that even among those who anticipated an ideal king in the lineage of David,

Jesus might not have seemed a likely candidate. After all, Jesus' kingship both adopted and adapted the tradition of expectation associated with the hoped-for son of David. Moreover, images and hopes other than those associated with a royal messiahship coalesced around his person.

According to Gabriel's annunciation to Mary regarding her son, Jesus is the royal Messiah, as we have seen; but, even within Luke's own writings, Jesus is also the prophet like Moses. "Listen to him," God instructs Peter, James, and John, who have gone up onto the Mount of Transfiguration with Jesus, where, we are told, Jesus discusses his "exodus" (Luke 9:28-36). In speaking thus, God echoes words spoken in Deuteronomy 18:15-18: "The LORD your God will raise up for you a prophet like me [Moses]. . . . You shall heed such a prophet." Indeed, these words of Deuteronomy are quoted by Peter in Acts 3:11-26, where they are said to have been fulfilled in Jesus. Elsewhere, too, the Jewish crowds are said to have responded to Jesus' great deeds by referring to him as the prophet who was to come (Luke 7:16; John 6:14). And without using the categories of messiahship, the New Testament Book of Hebrews refers to Jesus as a priest—indeed, as the unsurpassed high priest (4:14).

Clearly, more is at work in the presentation of Jesus in the New Testament than might be contained in the category of "fulfilling Jewish expectations of the Messiah." This is in part because those expectations were ill-defined and not held universally among Jewish people. It is also true because that category is too small. We may be on firmer ground if we shift the focus from particular titles and narrowly defined expectations to what is clearly central in Jesus' teaching—namely, the kingdom of God.

Jesus and the Kingdom of God

To speak of the "kingdom of God" is immediately to raise questions of language. First, no distinction can be drawn between the two phrases "kingdom of God" and "kingdom of heaven"; the two are used interchangeably, with the term *heaven* used as a substitute for "God" (com-

---

1,

Think about your own experiences of the Christmas season in recent years. Have Israel's ancient hopes for divine intervention and deliverance been reflected in your own thoughts and hopes? Please explain.

pare, for example, Matthew 13:11; Mark 4:11; Luke 8:10). Second, in recent decades, many within the church have objected to the use of the word *kingdom* as possessing inherently masculine connotations and have translated the Greek work *basileia* with the English word *reign* instead. This is unfortunate for two reasons: (1) The word *kingdom* possessed hierarchical and masculine connotations in Roman antiquity, but this did not keep Jesus from using the term and using it in ways that actually subverted those connotations. To say, as he did, that the kingdom of God belongs to little children was to raise serious and pervasive questions against common understandings of the term *kingdom* in his world. (2) "Kingdom" is more than "reign," for it also includes the notion of "realm." Translation of *basileia* as "reign" too easily allows us to reduce the work of God to his reign "in our hearts" or to those people among whom God reigns. In either case, the reach of the kingdom of God has been severely limited. Of course, the phrase "kingdom of God" has already been represented in new ways in the New Testament—as "life" in the Gospel of John, for example—and the church might do well to struggle in particular communities with how best to communicate its substance in contemporary language (God's new world order? The new era?). For the sake of this discussion, however, I will use the more traditional phrase, "kingdom of God."

That the message of Jesus can be summarized in terms of the kingdom of God (of the 103 references to the Kingdom in the Gospels, see especially Mark 1:14-15) points not only to the importance of the concept of the Kingdom in his ministry but also to the presumption of some prior knowledge of the Kingdom among Jesus' audience. This does not mean that Jesus' message was necessarily tied to popular definitions of the Kingdom, but it does suggest that he could employ the phrase with confidence that his audiences would have shared with him some general understanding of its significance.

We may therefore be surprised to discover that the phrase itself is absent from Israel's Scriptures. I should quickly add, though, that the portrait of God as king, which implies a kingdom, is important to Old Testament faith.

Particularly with the rise of the prophets Amos and Hosea in the eighth century B.C., the people of Israel turned their eyes to the future activity of God in history. For them, hope focused on the coming of the Lord in history as king. Later, Isaiah would describe the triumph of God as deliverer and sovereign in anticipation of the glorious reign of God (for example, Isaiah 24:23; 30:33; 32:1; 33:17, 20-22). This portrait of God is not restricted to the prophets, however. The concept of God as king is present in the earliest history of the nation, as God serves as deliverer, leader, and lawgiver in Israel's experience of exodus from Egypt and settlement in the Promised Land. Not surprisingly, the language of kingship surfaces most clearly in the period of the monarchy. Irrespective of what human king sat on Israel's throne, the true king was God; and it was God who defined faithful kingship. Then, in the Prophets, God's coming reign was announced as a symbol of Israel's renewal. In Isaiah's words, the good news of consolation is focused on the proclamation, "Here is your God!" (Isaiah 40:9) or, "Our God reigns" (Isaiah 52:7).

How would Jesus' contemporaries have understood the kingdom of God? There are three essential features. First, the kingdom of God entails the restoration of Israel; but it is not limited to Israel's national boundaries. In the end, God's kingdom is cosmic in its proportions. Thus, the restoration of Israel could not be a localized affair but somehow must address all the nations of the world. Second, the kingdom of God is nothing less than God coming to set things right. God's rule spells justice, the triumph of righteousness and establishment of peace in the world—shalom. This means that the kingdom of God can never be reduced to a "merely" spiritual affair, though it is at least this. All of life—friendships, social systems, home chores, business practices, shopping, international relations, and more— falls under the purview of the Kingdom. Third, the kingdom of God has to do with the coming *of God*. That is, anticipation of universal shalom was not necessarily tied to a messiah or messianic figure. To proclaim the arrival of the kingdom would be to announce the arrival of God himself to rule.

2,

What is the relationship of these expectations to the ministry of Jesus? Do these hopes find their fulfillment in the coming of Jesus? The only possible answer is equivocal: Yes *and* No. We must say Yes because this is precisely what the Gospels broadcast, that Jesus not only shared these expectations but also actually regarded them as realized in his ministry. "The long-awaited time has been fulfilled! The kingdom of God is at your fingertips!" (Mark 1:15; author's translation). What is more, in his ministry Jesus was not only the one who announced the kingdom but was also its bearer. Wherever Jesus was engaged in ministry, there the kingdom of God was at hand—present in his work, active through him personally. At the same time, we must answer No because Jesus did not perform in the expected way, at least not in the way expected by those texts that presumed a militaristic resolution. According to the Gospels of Matthew and Luke, even John the Baptist was baffled by the direction of Jesus' mission. Where was the anticipated fiery judgment on Israel's enemies (see Matthew 3:11-12; 11:2-3; Luke 3:16-17; 7:18-20)?

In what ways do you see the concerns reflected in biblical expectations related to the kingdom of God at work in the ministry of Jesus? in the ministries of your local church?

Christology, then, has its foundations in Jesus' understanding of his own place within the story of Israel, and specifically within the story of God's fidelity to his people. The time of restoration was at hand; evil was being rolled back; peace with justice was being established throughout the world; and God was present to rule—all in the ministry of Jesus, but not in ways commonly articulated among Jesus' contemporaries. For him, disclosure of the will of God meant standing at the threshold of fresh ways of conceiving God's work and stepping across it. Having done so, all the world would be different because one would be able to see it differently. No longer working at cross purposes with the ancient purpose of God, they would find themselves in sync with God's own aims and active in God's own redemptive project. The vision Jesus put forward thus addressed the central hopes of Israel but presented them in alternative dress. The hostility he attracted, which led inevitably to his death in Jerusalem, was the consequence of competing visions of God and God's work and rival ways of reading Israel's Scriptures. Jesus was engaged in a battle of perception and interpretation, one that had profound implications for what one believed and how one practiced faithfulness before God. The new exodus was underway, the new era was breaking in upon the old, and all of this was manifest in Jesus' person and work.

Jesus, God's Envoy

3.

In light of biblical expectations related to the kingdom of God, how might we understand Jesus' directive to "seek first the kingdom" (Matthew 6:33)?

According to one of the earliest Christian traditions we possess, "Christ died for our sins in accordance with the scriptures, and . . . he was buried, and . . . he was raised on the third day in accordance with the scriptures" (1 Corinthians 15:3-4).

Which scriptural texts find their fulfillment according to this traditional confession, cited by Paul? Where does one find in Israel's Bible that the Christ would die for our sins? Where in the Old Testament do we read that the Christ would be buried and raised on the third day? Of course, one might take on the scissors-and-paste task of putting together verses and fragments of verses in order to show that, in these events, Christ fulfilled the Scriptures. This misses the point, however. In these events, Jesus did not fulfill this or that scriptural text; rather, he fulfilled "the Scriptures."

Let me try to spell this point out by developing it along three different lines. First, we have evidence in this early creed that all of the Scriptures, and not only the specifically forward-looking segments, can be understood as "prophetic." The Scriptures of Israel interpret the past, to be sure; but even in doing so, they are oriented toward an end that remains future even when the last word of the last biblical book is written. They point beyond themselves to an end, or aim, so that in them we have a book of ever-increasing anticipation.

Second, the Scriptures are not merely records of Israel's engagement with the Lord. Rather, they give voice to God's ancient and eternal purposes. To affirm that the promises of the Scriptures have been actualized is to affirm that God's own aims are coming to pass. The phrase "according to the Scriptures" is thus a kind of shorthand, affirming that God's will has been realized. Consequently, the early Christian tradition Paul has written into his letter to Corinth does not single out a text of Scripture, or even some aspect of God's will; the Scriptures—that is, the purpose of God to which they give witness and the hope to which they point—have been fulfilled.

Third, God's purpose has been realized in Christ. It is not simply that Jesus has obeyed God's will and that events related to Jesus can be said to be fully aligned with God's will. More is at stake here. God's purpose, his fundamental aim in creation, has found completion in Christ.

In the end, this means that Christology is really theology. To speak of Christ is first to speak of God. What is accomplished in Christ is none other than God's doing.

---

[1] From "On the Incarnation," by Athanasius; 34.
[2] From "On the Incarnation," by Athanasius; 34.
[3] From "O Come, O Come, Emmanuel," in *The United Methodist Hymnal* (Copyright © 1989 The United Methodist Publishing House); 211.

3

The Spirit of Christmas

Key Concepts:
- Why do the four New Testament Gospels each begin the narrative of Jesus in a different way?
- Why is the role of the Holy Spirit in Jesus' mission so crucial?
- What do the writings of the New Testament mean when they refer to Jesus as "Son of God"?
- Why did God become a human?

Hark! the herald angels sing, 'Glory to the newborn King!' " Written in 1734, these words of Charles Wesley summarize well the witness of the Gospels of Matthew and Luke to the birth of Jesus. Although with different emphases, both secure Jesus within the lineage of David and present him as the royal Messiah. According to Matthew, astrologers (or magi) from the East even traveled to Jerusalem with the question, "Where is the child who has been born king of the Jews?" (Matthew 2:1-2). Further into Wesley's hymn, "Hark! The Herald Angels Sing," we find words that speak even more profoundly of the meaning of the first Christmas:

> Veiled in flesh the Godhead see;
> hail th' incarnate Deity.

Here Charles Wesley captured the central Christian claim that, in this newborn king, God disclosed himself. Christmas, then, is the coming of God.

How is God related to the universe and to the human family? What is God's character? What is his design for us? How does God make himself known to us? These "God questions" and others like them were defined ultimately and answered decisively in the advent of Jesus.

Our focus in this chapter is the meaning of Christmas. How do the Gospels tell the story of beginnings? In the birth of Jesus, what is the role and significance of Mary? of Joseph? of the Spirit of God? What is the relationship between Jesus' having been "conceived by the Holy Spirit," as the Apostles' Creed has it, and his being anointed with the Spirit at his baptism? When we speak of Jesus as "th' incarnate Deity," as God become flesh, what do we affirm in and about our faith as Christians?

The Problem of a Beginning

For those raised in the Christian faith, the narrative of Jesus' birth recorded in Luke's Gospel may be familiar territory. "In those days a decree went out from Emperor Augustus" (Luke 2:1). Even a casual comparison of the New Testament Gospels reveals that each begins its biography of Jesus in a different way. As with biographical literature in the Roman world in general, none of the Gospels has much to say about the birth and childhood of Jesus, formative influences on his early years, his growth into and beyond adolescence, or any of a number of other concerns that we now regard as interesting and significant for understanding a person's adult life. The Gospels of Mark and John have nothing to say about Jesus' birth whatsoever. Moreover, although Matthew and Luke speak of Jesus' birth and, to a lesser degree, infancy, their accounts have quite different beginning points and emphases. Why these differences?

In many aspects of life, making a beginning is difficult. "Where shall I begin?" we ask. This is especially true in biographical and historical narrative because the narrator struggles with the question, "How far back in the story must I go in order to make sense of the story itself?" Clearly, the writers of the New Testament Gospels, sometimes called Evangelists, answered this question in different ways. The Gospel of Matthew begins with a genealogy—not a particularly stimulating aspect of biblical literature for us and our contemporaries, but a highly important one for Matthew's. In many cultures, including the worlds of the Old Testament and the Roman Mediterranean, one's lineage was a potent marker of one's status. The question, "Who am I?" was asked and answered in terms of one's family and one's ancestral heritage. In a sense, Matthew claims that the story of Jesus, which he wants to tell, cannot be understood apart from an initial understanding of his parentage, and especially his relationship to Abraham and David. Only then is Matthew in a position to begin his account of Jesus' birth, which is seasoned generously with affirmations of divine intervention and direction and scriptural fulfillment.

Mark says nothing of Jesus' birth and only mentions Jesus' family well into the narrative, when Jesus returns to Nazareth to preach (Mark 6:1-6). But it is not true to say, as is often suggested, that Mark traces the story of Jesus back only to his baptism. Although it is true that Jesus' baptism is the first event Mark narrates, this is not where Mark begins his Gospel. Unfortunately, many modern translations camouflage Mark's interests by mistranslating the first three verses of Mark 1. For example, the NRSV reads, "The beginning of the good news of Jesus Christ, the Son of God" (Mark 1:1). This translation assumes that Mark's first verse functions as a kind of title for the book, when in fact Mark's text ties "the beginning of the good news" directly into what was written by the prophet Isaiah. A more appropriate translation would thus read,

> The beginning of the good news of Jesus Christ, the Son of God, as it stands written in the prophet Isaiah:
> "See, I am sending my messenger ahead of you, who will prepare your way;

> the voice of one crying out in the wilderness:
> 'Prepare the way of the Lord,
> make his paths straight.' " (Mark 1:1-3)

For Mark, then, the story of Jesus does not begin with his baptism but with the prophetic message of Isaiah. There, in Isaiah 40 (the larger context of the words Mark quotes), the "good news" is defined in terms of the coming of God to bring consolation to Israel. To open his narrative in this way, then, Mark claims from the outset that the advent of Jesus was nothing less than the coming of God to bring salvation. We are not surprised to hear Jesus' words in Mark 1:15, then, where "the good news of God" (Mark 1:14) is defined in terms of the arrival of God's kingdom.

Luke devotes a great deal of attention to the birth of Jesus, tying it, first, into his account of the birth of John the Baptist and, more profoundly, into God's promises to Abraham, which are now coming to fruition (Luke 1:5–2:52). A comparison of the material devoted to Abraham in Genesis 11–21 with Luke's account of the births of John and Jesus indicates how tightly interwoven these stories are, beginning with references to divine intervention in the lives of the righteous and continuing into the clear affirmation that, in the birth of Jesus, God's covenant with Abraham was coming to fruition. The promises to Abraham (see Genesis 12:3; 15:5, 13-14, 18-21; 17:2, 4-8), especially that he would be the father of many nations, are not only remembered but kept (see Luke 1:55, 73). For Luke, then, the story of Jesus cannot be understood apart from its location at the center of God's ancient purpose to bring salvation to the whole world through the people of Abraham.

In terms of identifying Jesus, the most prominent claim Luke emphasizes is Jesus' status as Son of God, which is announced by the angel Gabriel (Luke 1:32-35), embraced by the twelve-year-old Jesus (Luke 2:49), pronounced by God himself (Luke 3:21-22), then acknowledged (though tested!) by the devil (Luke 4:1-13). For Luke, as for Matthew, even the conception of Jesus was due to God's intervention, so that, in an important sense, the significance of Jesus can never be understood in or reduced to merely human terms.

The Gospel of John follows none of the possibilities we have discussed thus far. Instead, John initiates his narrative of Jesus' adult life and ministry with a kind of confessional statement or hymn (John 1:1-18). In this way he traces Jesus' beginnings, not to his baptism, not to his birth, not to scriptural promise, but to the eternal past. Echoing the words of Genesis, John writes, "In the beginning . . ." (John 1:1), then affirms that the Son of God, God's own Word (or *Logos*, the Greek term John uses), was God's agent of creation and, indeed, *was God*! In making this claim, John borrows several ideas from contemporary Jewish philosophical writings, including the pre-existence of the Word, the status of the Word as an agent of creation and medium of divine governance in the world, and the role of the Word as the means by which we know God. John thus uses ideas that would have been familiar to others in the larger Jewish and Gentile worlds; but in the midst of the familiar, he introduces an astonishing innovation. Verse 14 is stunning: "The Word became flesh and lived among us" (John 1:14). Here is John's affirmation of what we have learned to call the Incarnation—God become human or, in the words of Charles Wesley, "the Godhead" now in human flesh, "th' incarnate Deity." For John, then, the mural of Jesus' life is not complete unless it embraces all of eternity and the whole cosmos.

The four New Testament Gospels each orient us to the significance of Jesus' life in different ways, but all of them situate him squarely within the purpose of God. Can more be said of the nature of Jesus' birth and the Incarnation?

The Spirit and Gynecology

Although the most controversial aspect of the New Testament narratives of Jesus' birth is their representation of Jesus' birth as the consequence of a virginal conception, their primary emphasis actually falls elsewhere, on the importance of divine intervention and especially the role of the Holy Spirit. To put it bluntly, these narratives have more to do with pneumatology (our understanding of the Holy Spirit and his activity) than with gynecology. Let me explain.

Especially in the modern world, under the influence of Enlightenment thinking, the notion of Jesus' birth recounted in the Apostles' Creed ("conceived by the Holy Spirit, born of the Virgin Mary") is sometimes minimized, if not rejected outright. Of course, this idea was extraordinary in the first century as well. Witness Mary's words after hearing Gabriel's announcement: "How can this be, since I am a virgin?" (Luke 1:34). Ancient and modern sensibilities notwithstanding, the Gospel texts point clearly in this direction. In Matthew's Gospel, the crucial phrase is found in 1:18: "Before they [Mary and Joseph] lived together, she was found to be with child from the Holy Spirit." In ancient Judaism marriage consisted of three acts: betrothal (a binding engagement), payment of the "bride price," and consummation through sexual intimacy. That Mary and Joseph had not "lived together" is not simply a reference to cohabitation, therefore, but to sexual intercourse. Based on this phrase, we might imagine that Matthew is leaving open the possibility that Mary was pregnant through intercourse with someone other than Joseph, perhaps the victim of rape. This possibility is ruled out, however, by the addition of the phrase "from the Holy Spirit" (repeated in Matthew 1:20). Matthew affirms, thus, that Joseph could not have been Jesus' natural father and, without further explanation, that Mary's pregnancy was the result of the Holy Spirit's action.

Some readers of the Gospels imagine that accounts of Jesus' conception were modeled on mythological accounts in which a Greek or Roman god assumed human form and impregnated a female. In this case, the Holy Spirit provides the male seed for Jesus' conception. Matthew provides no hint of such an encounter, however; and neither does Luke. These Evangelists have nothing to say about God taking on human form in order to father a child. Unlike the ancient Greek myths, we read nothing in the New Testament of God appearing as a phantom human in disguise so as to have a sexual encounter with Mary. (Already in the second century A.D., Justin Martyr had distinguished the miraculous birth of Jesus from Greco-Roman myth.)

Luke is more forthcoming than Matthew, but even he writes only that "the Holy Spirit will come upon you, and the power of the Most High will overshadow you; therefore the child to be born will be holy; he will be called Son of God" (Luke 1:35). From this we learn that Jesus is the Son of God, not because he assumes the throne of David (see Psalm 2:7), but because of the miraculous nature of his conception. The verbs used in Gabriel's announcement, *to come upon* and *to overshadow*, are not particularly special or unique but speak elsewhere of empowerment (for example, Acts 1:8) and the manifestation of the glory of God (for example, Exodus 40:35; Numbers 9:18, 22). They affirm divine intervention but provide nothing by way of detail as to how we are to imagine this occurred. Other New Testament texts that might witness to the virginal conception of Jesus (Romans 1:3; Galatians 4:4; Philippians 2:7) add nothing to how we might understand the biology of Jesus' conception.

If Joseph belongs to David's ancestral line and if Jesus is not the natural son of Joseph, how can Jesus be the son of David? Again we encounter differences between cultures—ours versus theirs. To belong to a family in Roman antiquity was fundamentally a question of being recognized as such. DNA tests (even if they had been available) would not have been a factor. If Joseph recognized Jesus as his son (and thus within the royal lineage of David), then legally this made it so.

Although affirmations of the virginal conception do not pepper the pages of the New Testament, the virginal conception of Jesus is nonetheless important for the way it underscores the uniqueness of Jesus among other human beings. His origins were with God; even in his conception he was the gracious gift of God. As the Nicene Creed has it, the character of Jesus' birth is thus linked with the doctrine of the Incarnation: "incarnate of the Holy Spirit and the Virgin Mary." And as Ignatius wrote in the early second century A.D., it was in the birth of Jesus that "God appeared in human form."[1]

1.

Reflect for a few minutes on the Christmas story. What does this story tell us about humanity? about God?

Before discussing the Incarnation more directly, the crucial role of the Holy Spirit in Christology should be mentioned further. The angel of the Lord, Gabriel, had prophesied that John the Baptist, while already in the womb, would be filled with the Spirit (Luke 1:15). As important as this is, however, Gabriel went further in his description of Jesus, attributing Jesus' very being to the Spirit (1:32-35). Within the world of Jewish reflection on the Holy Spirit, what Gabriel promised was extraordinary; but it was not without analogy. After all, we find in the literature of Second Temple Judaism that the Spirit of the Lord was regularly credited with the power of miracles, creation, and even resurrection.

If we expand our thinking further, we may see an immediate connection between Jesus' messiahship and his experience of the Spirit. "Messiah," we may recall, refers to "anointing." In the Old Testament, this was an anointing with oil, whereby a person was set apart for divine service as a priest or king. Jesus received no such oil anointing but is nonetheless regarded as the Anointed One. This is related directly to his having been anointed with the Spirit at his baptism. Indeed, in his sermon at Nazareth, as Luke reports it, Jesus interpreted his baptism by claiming for himself the prophetic words of Isaiah:

> The Spirit of the Lord is upon me,
> because he has anointed me.
> He has sent me to bring good news to the poor:
> to proclaim release to the captives
>   and recovery of sight to the blind,
> to let the oppressed go free,
> to proclaim the year of the Lord's favor.
> (Luke 4:18-19, citing Isaiah 61:1-2; 58:6;
> author's translation of Isaiah)

Within the Gospel of Luke, this citation points backward and forward—backward to the baptism of Jesus and forward to the character of his mission. At Jesus' baptism, "the Holy Spirit descended upon him"; and God affirmed, "You are my Son" (Luke 3:21-22). In this way, Jesus' iden-

How pivotal would you say Jesus' experience of the Spirit was to his sense of identity and mission? Has your experience of the Spirit been important in similar ways?

tity as God's Son and his empowerment by the Holy Spirit were intertwined in a way that would prove decisive throughout his ministry. In his person and ministry Israel's expectations, centered on the outpouring of the Spirit to bring restoration to Israel, came to fulfillment. Jesus' experience of the Spirit, then, was the necessary presupposition of his mission. Looking even further forward, the Spirit's anointing of Jesus at his baptism prepared for the outpouring of the Spirit at Pentecost (Acts 2). In this way the messianic community of Jesus' followers was empowered by the Spirit to share in and extend his ministry.

The Divinity of Jesus: A Cautionary Comment

The issue of what constitutes evidence for the divinity of Jesus may puzzle some Christians. Many of us have assumed that the titles given him in the New Testament—especially "Christ," "Lord," and "Son of God"—all mark Jesus in some important sense as God. This is not necessarily the case, however.

Consider, for example, the affirmation of Jesus as the Son of God, shared by all the Gospels, Paul, Hebrews, First John, and Revelation. If Jesus is God's Son, does this not necessitate Jesus' deity? An important way to address this question is to ask, How might first-century Jews and Gentiles have heard this title? In Israel's Scriptures this phrase is used to describe the people of Israel (see Exodus 4:22-23; Hosea 11:1), for example, or the reigning king on Israel's throne (see 2 Samuel 7:14; Psalm 89:26-27). In neither case do connotations of divinity apply; rather, sonship is understood more in terms of representation and (hoped for) obedience. The idea of being chosen by God for particular service is also present. In the Old Testament, angels might also be known as "sons of God" (see Genesis 6:2; Daniel 3:25).

The situation in the larger Roman world was not much different. When Julius Caesar died, his adopted son, whom we know from Luke's Gospel as Caesar Augustus, designated him as "a god," which made Augustus a "son of God." But this was not a claim to divinity on the part of Augustus. In fact, throughout his imperial rule, Augustus resisted attempts in the eastern part of his empire to divinize him. In the Roman world, "sonship" comprised three related emphases: The son represented his father and was obedient to him, and the father was responsible to carry out the education of his son.

It may be of further interest that, in ways that were more common in antiquity than today, to be a "child" of something or someone was to share that thing or person's characteristics. John the Baptist played on this idea when he warned people not to think of themselves as "children of Abraham" simply because they could trace their ancestry to Abraham. Instead, they should see themselves as Abraham's "children" if they represented in their lives his fidelity to God. By way of analogy, as God's Son, Jesus would represent in his own life God's character; but the evidence available to us does not allow us to conclude simply from the designation of Jesus as God's Son that he was divine.

There is no evidence at all in the Judaism of Jesus' day to lead us to imagine that the title "Christ" carried with it connotations of divinity, but the situation with the term *lord* is somewhat more complicated. This is because the title was used throughout the Roman Empire not simply as a term of polite address (as is often claimed) but also as a way of addressing one's superior and, especially, one's patron. To refer to the emperor as "lord," then, was to recognize his status as the patron of the whole Empire, the benefactor of all, to whom allegiance and honor were due. Similarly, to refer to Jesus as "Lord" would be to recognize him as the one through whom God's gracious gifts of healing and salvation are available. In the first century, to call Jesus "Lord" may well have been a way of countering claims made on behalf of the Roman emperor. Of course, the Greek version of Israel's Bible sometimes uses the term *kyrios* ("lord") to refer to God; and we may assume that Jesus' status as "lord" reflected that usage among Christians whose thoughts and vocabulary were steeped in the Scriptures. At times this title must have designated Jesus as the one to whom Christians owed their redemption and thus their allegiance, as God's singular agent of salvation. At other times, however,

Christians must have used the term in its even more exalted sense, with the effect that Jesus was even more directly and fully associated with God.

Titles allotted to Jesus by early Christians, then, provide no necessary or direct witness to Jesus' divinity. Neither do his miracles. It is often said that Jesus' divinity was demonstrated in his miraculous activity, as recorded in the Gospels. A text like Acts 2:22 indicates certainly that the signs and wonders Jesus performed identified him as God's agent; but it is important that, in this text, we read that God worked those powerful deeds through Jesus. In this light, we may recall that the Scriptures report other workers of miracles (the prophets Elijah and Elisha, for example, or in the New Testament, Stephen and Paul); yet, we do not regard these persons as divine on this account.

With regard to the miracle tradition, some details of Jesus' regular practices are of further interest, however. Although the Greek and Jewish worlds spoke of persons like Jesus who performed miracles, no one was presented as working miracles in the way that Jesus did. That is, whereas some healers might pray to God for healing or others might involve themselves in complex rites and incantations, Jesus often simply pronounced a person's healing. "Young man, I say to you, rise!" (Luke 7:14). "Be healed of your disease!" (Mark 5:34). With such pronouncements as these, Jesus acted as though he possessed in himself the authority and power to heal; and this surely has implications for how we understand his person.

Incarnation and Discipleship

Affirmations of the Incarnation litter the pages of apostolic writers in the period just after the New Testament materials were written. In the first decade of the second century, Ignatius wrote of Jesus, "There is one Physician who is possessed both of flesh and spirit. He is both made and not made. He is God existing in flesh, true Life in death. He is both of Mary and of God."[2] Some seventy-five years later, Irenaeus asserted that "his advent according to the flesh was the thing by which the blending and communion of God and humanity took place."[3] Apart from the Gospel of John, evidence within the New Testament is less explicit than these straightforward affirmations; but it is plentiful.

John's Gospel, as we have noted, has it that the eternal Word became flesh and dwelled among us (John 1:1-14). Elsewhere too, the divinity of Jesus is affirmed in this Gospel, such as when the divine name "I AM" (see Isaiah 51:12; 52:6) is assigned to Jesus (for example, John 8:24, 28, 58; 13:19). In Hebrews, Creation is said to have been accomplished through the agency of God's Son (Hebrews 1:1-3; see also Colossians 1:15-16); and First John is evidently concerned in part with people who think of Jesus as divine but not as having actually become a human (1 John 4:1-4; see 2 John 7). Evidence for the divinity of Jesus in New Testament thought also appears in the fact that he was worshiped (for example, Revelation 5). Paul does not so much assert the Incarnation as assume it (for example, 2 Corinthians 8:9). In a text in Philippians notable for its Christological content, however, the Incarnation is on full display. Paul speaks of Jesus Christ

> who, though he was in the form of God,
>> did not regard equality with God
>> as something to be exploited,
> but emptied himself,
>> taking the form of a slave,
>> being born in human likeness.
> And being found in human form,
>> he humbled himself
>> and became obedient to the point of death—
>> even death on a cross.
>
> Therefore God also highly exalted him
>> and gave him the name that is above every
>>> name,
> so that at the name of Jesus
>> every knee should bend,
>> in heaven and on earth and under the earth,
> and every tongue should confess

that Jesus Christ is Lord,
to the glory of God the Father.

(Philippians 2:6-11)

In this poetic passage, Paul presents Christology as the journey of Christ—from his existence "in the form of God" to his taking on "human form" and from his obedience even to the point of death to his exaltation as Lord. We should not be put off by Paul's use of the term *form*, as though this meant something other than the reality of his existence. After all, Jesus, Paul confirms, was in the "form" of humanity just as he was in the "form" of God. This leads to the simple conclusion that Paul presents Jesus as having existed **before** the creation of the cosmos and as possessing **equality** with God.

What is being affirmed in language of this nature? First, the language of pre-existence provides us with an important way of speaking of Jesus as the revelation of the eternal God. As "truly God and truly human," Jesus both represents the historical realities of human existence in all its frailty and specificity and discloses a reality that transcends the cosmos and is, indeed, eternal. The Word that became flesh is from "the beginning" (John 1:1). Second, the language of pre-existence reminds us that the significance of Jesus' mission, and especially his mission to restore Israel, can never be limited to a particular historical moment or people. If, as Revelation 1:8 has it, Jesus is the "Alpha and the Omega," the first and the last, then the salvation he brings and the way of faithful life he reveals cannot be reduced to the late first century or to Galilee. Third, Jesus is the decisive manifestation of God; here we see who God is and what God is like. In this, Jesus has no competitors. Fourth, the coming of Jesus was no divine afterthought but was already resident in the purpose of God from the beginning; hence, the salvation he brings is nothing less than the fellowship of God, humanity, and the cosmos for which God expressed himself in Creation in the first place. As the writer of Hebrews has it, the Incarnation is the climax of a long historical process: "Long ago God spoke to our ancestors in many and varied ways by the prophets, but in these

3.

The doctrine of the Incarnation is central to classical Chrisian faith. What is its significance to your understanding of faithful discipleship?

last days he has spoken to us by the Son, whom he appointed heir of all things, through whom he also created the worlds" (Hebrews 1:1-2).

The Incarnation is God's ultimate self-disclosure. As "Word made flesh," Jesus is in a unique position to represent God to humanity and humanity to God, so as to mediate between God and humanity and to bring peace where before there was separation. These are crucial affirmations that go to the very heart of the Christian faith. To these, one more affirmation must be added. This is that the Incarnation provides the ground and content of faithful life before God. We might refer to this as the "ethical" importance of the Incarnation. In order to grasp this idea, consider the problem addressed in First John. Apparently, John was faced with persons who denied that the Son of God was really a human being and who therefore lived lives marked by disobedience toward God and lack of love toward others. That is, if God's Son did not really become human, then life in this world has no lasting consequence. But if God's Son has become human, then this means that human beings, and with them all creation, are embraced in God's care and concern and life in this world is of the utmost importance. Therefore, John insists, those who are genuine members of God's family are well-known because they "walk just as he walked" and love one another (1 John 2:6; 4:7-8). Their lives are marked by holy love.

Interestingly, other New Testament writers speak of the Incarnation in similar ways. They are not interested in Jesus' pre-existence or in the Incarnation as questions of speculative philosophy; rather, they employ this profound Christological statement in order to call forth from their audiences lives of significance and faithfulness. For John's Gospel, the journey of Jesus from his pre-existent glory to his earthly ministry leads to the washing of the feet of the disciples—an act that ought to be replicated among his followers as they eschew concerns with status and pride and place themselves in positions of genuine service toward one another (John 13). Paul included the poetic text cited above (Philippians 2:6-11) as a case study in attitudes and behaviors that fund genuine community among believers.

Let your lives be marked by humility, he urges. Look to the interests of other people rather than to your own. And "let the same mind be in you that was in Christ Jesus" (Philippians 2:1-5). Here the Incarnation is a model for relating to others with open-handed graciousness. Give generously, Paul writes elsewhere; "for you know the generous act of our Lord Jesus Christ, that though he was rich, yet for your sakes he became poor, so that by his poverty you might become rich" (2 Corinthians 8:9).

These are not speculative treatises on the incarnation of the Son of God. We find in the New Testament no concern with theoretical formulations of the divine-human nature of Jesus or of the pre-existence of the Son of God. The Incarnation is affirmed, to be sure, as are the humanity and divinity of Jesus. But these affirmations are made in terms of what they imply for our salvation, for the restoration of the whole cosmos to God, and for the character of life before God. God became human so that we might live in fellowship with him and so that we might know the nature of life lived in fellowship with him.

[1] From *Epistle to the Ephesians,* by Ignatius; 19:3.
[2] From *Epistle to the Ephesians,* by Ignatius; 7.
[3] From *Against Heresies,* by Irenaeus; 20:4.

4

Jesus, the (New) Human

Key Concepts:

- What evidence does the New Testament present for the humanness of Jesus?
- What does it mean to be created in the "image of God"?
- How does Jesus demonstrate "authentic humanity"?
- What is the significance of the contrast Paul draws between the "first Adam" and the "last Adam"?

In A.D. 451, the great ecumenical Council of Chalcedon produced a landmark statement of classical Christian faith concerning the person of Jesus. "We all unanimously teach," those gathered affirmed, "that we should confess that our Lord Jesus Christ is one and the same Son; the same perfect in Godhead and the same perfect in humanity, truly God and truly human." Both sides of the equation are crucial, the divinity of Jesus and his humanity. The latter may seem obvious; indeed, in recent years, it is the divinity of Jesus (including affirmations of the pre-existence of the Son and the Incarnation) that has come under increased scrutiny. Jesus' humanity is so often taken for granted that its importance for our faith and life as Christians is rarely understood.

One way to emphasize the importance of Jesus' humanity is to insist that Christology is first anthropology. That is,

Jesus first demonstrates to us the nature of true humanity, human existence according to God's original purpose in creating the human family. What is more, Jesus opens the way for a new humanity, in which the bent toward sinning characteristic of Adam's race no longer enslaves us so that we are freed for holiness and love.

According to the Gospel of Matthew (1:21-23), Mary's son is to bear two names. The first is "Jesus" ("for he will save his people from their sins"); how Jesus saves is the topic for later chapters. The second is "Emmanuel" (which means "God is with us"). Depending on where one places the emphasis, "Emmanuel" could be an affirmation of the presence of *God* with us or the presence of God with *us*. In this chapter, our focus will be on the latter, on the fullness of Jesus' humanity.

Jesus Was Truly a Human

Though they were quite capable of portraying Jesus with reference to his uniqueness and in exalted terms, the writers of the New Testament also devoted attention to his experience as a human. The extraordinary character of his conception aside, Jesus, like every other human being, was born of a woman; and like every other Jew, he was born under the law (Galatians 4:4). He shared a human pedigree (see Luke 3:23-38; Romans 1:3). Some evidence suggests that Jesus' birth was regarded as unusual even by people of his hometown. He may well have been regarded as illegitimate (see Mark 6:3; John 8:41). If this reputation followed Jesus in his childhood and adolescence, this would suggest his solidarity with all humans who have experienced the ridicule of being labeled and ostracized.

Luke stresses as well that Jesus experienced the normal processes of maturation: "Jesus increased in wisdom and in years, and in divine and human favor" (Luke 2:52). Such a claim would have been quite extraordinary, not least among those who regarded Jesus as divine or even as an admirable public figure. Our contemporary notions of social and emotional development are alien to Roman antiquity, where public figures were assumed to have possessed even as children the qualities esteemed in adults. Among some later theologians, the notion that Jesus could increase in wisdom or that God's favor toward the child could increase proved problematic as well. What additional wisdom would the Son of God need that he did not already possess? How could God favor Jesus more with the passing of the years? Here again is poignant testimony to the affirmation that Jesus was "fully human."

If we can read back from the Gospel narratives of Jesus' adulthood, we may assume that in his earlier years Jesus was an avid reader of Scripture and that he nurtured his life before God in prayer, through Scripture, and in regular attendance in the synagogue. During his public ministry, he seemed to breathe the air of exemplary Jewish piety and to draw on the Scriptures as though he had grown intimate with them. The Gospels also portray Jesus as a person with a wide range of human emotions and needs: hunger, thirst, fatigue, astonishment, sorrow, joy, anger, and compassion. He devoted himself to a small circle of friends and desired companionship with them, prayed for guidance, experienced trials and temptations, and even acknowledged the limits of his own knowledge (for example, Mark 13:32). The Gospels also portray Jesus as sharing in the human condition of finiteness. He could not be everywhere and could not help everyone; he had to make choices. But he did so in ways consistent with prayerful consideration of his mission (for example, Luke 4:42-44).

According to the writer of Hebrews, in order to bring deliverance to humanity, in order to repeal the power of evil, it was necessary that Jesus share our human existence (2:14). Paul confirms that Christ's birth "in human likeness" (Philippians 2:7) was essential to his journey to bring salvation.

Jesus Demonstrates True Humanity

The humanity of Jesus was not only realized in his experience of the human condition. If this were the case, then Jesus would be no different than his contemporaries and other humans before and after. Adam and Eve, according to Genesis 1–3, were created in the image of God; and with them so were all members of the human family. They were fully human, but they were not truly human. That is, they did not fulfill the purpose for which humanity was created by God, namely, to reflect the image of God in their lives. Instead, they chose to grasp at divinity themselves. What is a true human? According to the Book of Genesis, our embodied existence as human beings has this as its singular vocation: to reflect the image of God. Unlike other members of creation, animate and inanimate, humanity is created by God "in his own image":

> Then God said, "Let us make humankind in our image, according to our likeness; and let them have dominion over the fish of the sea, and over the birds of the air, and over the cattle, and over all the wild things of the earth, and over every creeping thing that creeps upon the earth."
> So God created humanity in his image,
> in the image of God he created them;
> male and female he created them.
> God blessed them, and God said to them, "Be fruitful and multiply, and fill the earth and subdue it; and have dominion over the fish of the sea and over the birds of the air and over every living thing that moves upon the earth." (Genesis 1:26-27)

Of all the creatures, only humanity is created after God's own likeness, in God's own image (*imago Dei*). Only to humanity does God speak directly. Humanity alone receives from God this divine vocation.

On this matter, the Genesis text is succinct, but not altogether forthcoming on interpretive detail. As a result, the tradition of interpretation of the "image of God" has been the focus of diverse understandings among Jews and Christians—ranging from some physical characteristic of humans (such as standing upright) to a way of knowing (especially the human capacity to know God) and so on. Taken within its immediate setting in Genesis 1, "the image of God" in which humanity is made most transparently relates to the exercise of dominion over the earth on God's behalf. But this observation only begs the question; for we must then ascertain what it means to exercise dominion in this way—that is, in a way that reflects God's own style of interaction with his creatures. What is more, this way of putting the issue does not grapple with the profound word spoken over humanity and about humanity, that human beings in themselves (and not only in what they do) reflect the divine image.

What is this quality that distinguishes humanity? God's words affirm the creation of the human family in its relation to him, as his counterpart, so that the nature of humanity derives from the human family's relatedness to God. The concept of the "image of God," then, is fundamentally relational and takes as its ground and focus the graciousness of God's own covenantal relations with humanity and the rest of creation. Humanity is created uniquely in relationship to God and finds itself as a result of creation in covenant with God. Humanity is given the divine mandate to reflect God's own covenant love in relation with God, within the covenant community of all humanity, and with all that God has created.

Outside of Genesis, creation "in the image of God" otherwise plays little role in the Old Testament, though it is mentioned in Second Temple Judaism. In the New Testament, Paul's thought is closest to the interpretation of the *imago Dei* expressed in the Wisdom of Solomon, wherein the phrase is used with reference to the actual expression of the "image of God" in a human life (rather than to human capacity or potential). Paul develops the motif of Christ as the "image of God" (2 Corinthians 4:4; Colossians 1:15; compare Philippians 2:6) and, as its corollary, the conformation of human beings into the image of Christ (Romans 8:29; 1 Corinthians 15:49; 2 Corinthians 3:18). Accordingly, "in Christ" believers have access to the ultimate purpose of God for humanity set forth in the creation of human life. Through his creative and reconciling activity and in his ethical comportment, Christ both reveals the nature of God and manifests truly the human vocation (compare Luke 6:35-36).

Christian theology has emphasized the triune nature of

1.

Have you ever considered that salvation entails nothing less than our being restored to authentic humanity? How might such a vision affect the way we think about mission and evangelism?

God, that is, the fundamental relatedness of God within the Godhead. Father, Son, and Holy Spirit—these constitute the community of the Godhead from which all revelation flows and on the basis of which all creation exists and has its meaning. The human person, understood as an individual, is not a reflection of the Godhead, as though the human person were complete in her- or himself. God's words at the creation of humankind were not spoken over a human person but over the human family. In fact, according to the Genesis text, God (singular) created humanity (singular) as men and women (plural), as "them" (plural). We do not reflect the community of the triune God as individuals but as the human community, whose life is differentiated from and yet bound up with nature and whose common life springs from and finds its end in God's embrace.

"Humanness," in this sense, is realized in and modeled by Jesus Christ. This is what it means to say that Jesus was both truly a human and that Jesus demonstrates true humanity.

This affirmation of Jesus' authentic humanity is closely linked to Jesus' being without sin. Matthew reports that Jesus "fulfill[ed] all righteousness" (3:15); while Hebrews observes that Jesus was holy, blameless, pure (7:26), tempted, but without sin (4:15). A closer look at this idea in Hebrews is in order.

The perspective of Hebrews is that the Old Testament is incomplete in itself and that the Old Testament actually points beyond itself, warning its readers not to make themselves too much at home there. One of its inadequacies is that its prescribed means for dealing with sin, the priesthood and sacrifice, were incapable of leading persons on to the desired goal of perfection. This is overcome in Jesus in two ways. First, he is both the perfect priest and the perfect sacrifice, so that his self-offering can deal with human sinfulness once and for all. Second, he is the trailblazer or pioneer of human salvation who opens up the path of perfect faithfulness. What does "perfect" mean in this New Testament book? Clearly, moral goodness is included; but "perfection" cannot be limited to moral goodness in Hebrews. This is because Jesus, though "holy, blameless, undefiled, separated from sinners" as he was (7:26), had still to become perfect (2:10; 5:7-9; 7:28). In this context, "perfect" has to do with Jesus' character, dispositions, and commitments; but it also has to do with his becoming fully qualified for the task laid before him. The central issue is that Jesus, if he is to be the pioneer of salvation, must be like other humans in every respect, including the full experience of suffering and temptation, and yet walk faithfully the path of obedience to God. This, according to the unknown writer of Hebrews, is exactly what Jesus did. What is more, if he is to open up the road of obedience that others might follow, he must do so with no more power at his disposal than would be available to those who would come after him. Like them (us!), he must live by faith and prayer, entrusting himself to the God who is able to save him (5:7).

Other perspectives might be heard. For example, the first three Gospels all agree that Jesus not only survived the onslaught of the devil's testing (and not only survived with his sense of identity and mission intact) but also actually overcame temptation through his faith in the sufficiency of God (see, for example, Matthew 4:1-11). What becomes clear from the New Testament evidence is that Jesus embodied fully the human vocation to reflect the image of God in all aspects of his life. Essential to his humanity was his sense and cultivation of the presence of God. Jesus practiced his humanity in relationship to others, and especially in extending relationship to those who lived outside the norms of acceptable society, the least and the last. He gathered around him a community of followers with and among whom he experienced "family" (see, for example, Luke 8:19-21). His experience of authentic humanity included his keen awareness of God's care for all creation, so much so that he could refer to grass and sparrows as case studies in the graciousness of God. As the Christ, Jesus is the true human.

Jesus Inaugurates a New Humanity

Pivotal for the work of salvation is that, in Christ, God identifies fully with humanity. It is also crucial that God be fully present to and for the human family. Jesus, then, not

2.

"Perfection" is an important concept in our Christian tradition, but it is not easily understood. As you reflect on the journey of Jesus as this has been sketched in this chapter, in general terms how would you describe "perfection"? What would "perfection" look like in your own life?

only entered into the human condition and demonstrates for all time the nature of authentic human existence but also opened the way for a new order of human life. He could do this only because he was fully human; but without this, his authentic humanity has no bearing on our lives. What good is a model, even one sent by God, if we are incapable of emulating it?

In his letters to the Romans and the Corinthians, Paul explores most profoundly the role of Jesus as the founder of a new humanity (see especially Romans 5:12-21; 1 Corinthians 15:21-22, 45-49). Here he works out the relationship between the first Adam (of the Genesis narrative) and the last Adam, Jesus. Paul's logic is simple: Adam represents the human race on a journey from life to death, while Christ represents humanity through death to life.

Accordingly, the old humanity is characterized by weakness. Following in the footsteps of Adam, humanity possesses an inescapable dimension of rebellion: sin. Humans not only fail to live up to their true humanity but also actually reject authentic humanity as a worthy goal. Refusing to embrace relationship with God as integral to human life, humanity instead grasps after "Godlikeness." Refusing to admit the finitude of human existence and therefore the utter necessity of interdependence with other humans and with nature, the human being falls far short of what he or she might have become. Choosing friendship with the world rather than friendship with God, humans end up with only a façade of their genuine selves and actually fail to live in harmony with the world within which they were created. This is the way of the first Adam.

Paul writes, however, that "as all die in Adam, so all will be made alive in Christ" (1 Corinthians 15:22). In Christ, a new humanity is thus possible and, indeed, has already been inaugurated. In this new humanity, old barriers are overcome. The dividing walls have been razed (see Ephesians 2:11-22). "There is no longer Jew or Greek, there is no longer slave or free, there is no longer male and female; for all of you are one in Christ Jesus" (Galatians 3:28).

In the late second century A.D., Tertullian wrote con-

3.

"I'm only human!" we sometimes say. How does the perspective on "humanity" embodied in this expression compare with the portrait of "humanity" available to us in the life of Jesus?

cerning the opposition faced by Christians, "It is mainly the deeds of a love so noble that lead many to put a brand upon us. They say, 'See how they love one another!' . . . And they are angry with us too because we call each other brothers."[1] Tertullian thus gave witness to the new community being formed in relationship to Jesus. Here were people whose lives with one another were genuinely reflecting God's own love for us.

Where did they learn thus to love one another and to embrace one another as though they were family? How were they enabled to see beyond their differences of culture and opinion in order to express love in a way that attracted the attention of those outside the church? All of this is grounded in the humanity of Jesus. As the true human, Jesus demonstrates what it means to live an authentically human life before God. As the founder of a new humanity, Jesus shows the way and empowers others to follow him in a community of reconciliation and care. And all of this is possible—Jesus can serve as our model, guide, and enabler—because in him God is fully identified with his people and fully present for them.

[1] From *Apology*, by Tertullian; 39.

5

The Mission of the Messiah

Key Concepts:
- What distinguishes the three stages of the quest of the historical Jesus?
- Why did Jesus adopt images of health care in describing his ministry?
- Who are the "poor" to whom Jesus addresses good news?
- How did Jesus undermine politics as usual in the Roman world?
- How would you summarize the "mission of the Messiah"?

The Apostles' Creed moves directly from Jesus' birth to his death:

> Conceived by the Holy Spirit,
> born of the Virgin Mary,
> suffered under Pontius Pilate,
> was crucified, dead, and buried.

The creed thus bypasses the messianic mission of Jesus, which was inaugurated at the time of his baptism and his anointing with the Spirit. In this respect the creed assumes a great deal, since the question is immediately raised, Why could someone whom we confess as "Jesus Christ, God's only Son, our Lord" find himself on a Roman cross? What is the relationship between miraculous conception and heinous death? In Chapter 6, I want to show how Jesus' death is the consequence of the life he lived in obedience to God. By way of preparing for that discussion, I want in this chapter to set forth more clearly the nature of Jesus' mission.

One way to ask this question is to inquire into the purpose of the Incarnation. Why did Jesus come? For what mission was he anointed by the Spirit?

What Can We Know of Jesus?

At the beginning of the twenty-first century, the questions before us will seem naive to some. A good bit of historical study in recent decades has encouraged increasing pessimism regarding the confidence with which we might speak about the nature of Jesus' life and mission.

What can we know of Jesus? Although it has only recently come into the public eye, this question is an old one. In the years following the Enlightenment, a new form of New Testament study surfaced, one that focused on the distinction between "what the Gospels say happened" and "what really happened." Study undertaken along these lines falls under the rubric of the "quest of the historical Jesus" and is usually divided into three stages.

The "First Quest" of the historical Jesus can be traced from the late eighteenth century to the turn of the twentieth, with beginnings usually dated to the posthumous publication of an essay by H.S. Reimarus (1694–1768) entitled "On the Intention of Jesus and His Disciples" in 1778. Here was the first in a long series of attempts to salvage a historically plausible picture of Jesus from a collection of writings, the New Testament Gospels, whose supernaturalism, it was alleged, could never be accepted by rational people. The First Quest had two defining characteristics: an unassailable confidence in human reason and a commitment to divorcing religion (or theology) from history. Unfortunately, the First Quest promised far more than it could deliver. Rather than giving us "Jesus as he really was," these studies tended to produce portraits of Jesus that looked surprisingly similar to those engaged in the study.

With the turn of the twentieth century, lives of Jesus continued to be written; but serious study no longer occupied the mainstream of New Testament research. Some refer to this as the period of "No Quest." These years were heavily influenced by Rudolf Bultmann, who taught that it was both impossible and unnecessary to know anything about the life of Jesus of Nazareth, apart from the mere fact (that is, the "that") that he lived. Authentic faith can never rest on historical research, Bultmann insisted; for then it would no longer be faith. What is needed instead is an encounter with the Christ of Christian proclamation. Some of Bultmann's own students countered this perspective by pursuing in fresh ways the question of continuity between the man from Nazareth who proclaimed the Kingdom and the Christ proclaimed by the early church. Such interests fueled the New Quest, or "Second Quest," of the historical Jesus.

At the turn of the twentieth century, Ernst Troeltsch proposed three principles for engaging in historical study; and these became axiomatic in the New Quest. First, he insisted on the principle of doubt: All statements of an historical nature are open to doubt and require substantiation. The second was the principle of analogy: Events in the ancient world follow the same internal logic as events in the modern world. Hence, for example, if we do not see people walking on water today, then by analogy we would conclude that the Gospel record of Jesus walking on water could not be accurate from a historical perspective. Third, Troeltsch (following the physical laws devised by Isaac Newton) posited the principle of correlation: Every event in the natural world is the result of (that is, must be correlated with) a natural cause. The possibility of a miracle was in this manner ruled out of court as a presupposition in historical inquiry.

By way of implementing these principles, participants in the New Quest developed a series of criteria honed to demonstrate for each of the sayings or actions attributed to Jesus in the Gospels either authenticity or inauthenticity. In this way they continued to speak in terms of peeling back the layers of theological interpretation in the Gospels in order to recover the historical kernel of those accounts. Armed with ever more precise instruments for engaging in such cutting and slicing, scholars in the Second Quest continued to think of history and theology in opposition. Chief among the criteria employed in the New Quest were two: dissimilarity and multiple attestation. The criterion of dissimilarity gives a bias in favor of authenticity to those traditions about Jesus that are incongruent with Jewish tradition and with the early church. To put it more crassly, the authentic Jesus emerges at those points where he is neither influenced by the Judaism of his world nor influential among his circle of disciples. This is the primary criterion utilized by the much-publicized "Jesus Seminar." In the last two decades of the twentieth century, this group of scholars met regularly to discuss the materials in the Gospels and especially to cast their votes whether what the Gospels report about Jesus' words and deeds can be taken as representing what Jesus actually said and did. The results were negative in the extreme; for example, the Gospel of Mark was determined to represent accurately what Jesus said in only one instance (Mark 12:17). Unfortunately, the publicity attracted by the Seminar was all out of proportion to its members' influence among other New Testament scholars.

The second of the two main criteria, multiple attestation, calls to mind images of the courtroom, with witness after witness called to the stand to report on an event. In study of Jesus, a tradition about Jesus would be regarded as authentic if testimony to it came from multiple, independent sources. The fundamental historicity of Jesus' instruction on "service," for example, might be supported with reference to the saying in Mark 10:45 ("The Son of Man came not to be served but to serve."), his parabolic teaching in Luke 12:35-38 (When the master returns from the wedding banquet, he will serve those who are faithful.), and the foot-washing scene in John 13:1-17.

Not surprisingly, the Second Quest made almost nothing of Jesus the Jew; nor did it have much to say about the continuity between Jesus and the church or between the historical Jesus and the church's Lord. What is surprising, perhaps, is that in spite of its so-called precision instruments and claims of objectivity, the New Quest also proved incapable of spawning a single portrait of the historical Jesus on which all could agree. Its most notable legacy was its skepticism about our potential for knowing anything about Jesus of Nazareth, not the historical certainty regarding him that it had sought.

Beginning in the late 1970's and continuing into the present is a "Third Quest" of the historical Jesus. What immediately distinguishes this one from its predecessors is its more realistic notion of history writing. On the one hand, aspects of life that were divorced from one another in historical study—for example, politics, religious experience, and economics—are now increasingly seen as integrated aspects of social existence. Similarly, the reporting of historical events is increasingly seen as an interpretive, even theological, enterprise. To use the previous analogy, whereas the New Quest sought to peel back the layers of theology to recover the historical core of the Gospel accounts, in the Third Quest it is increasingly granted that no layer is devoid of either history or theology.

These fresh perspectives have led to two related developments. First, the Gospels can be studied each on their own terms as coherent narratives, with each providing a plausible, theologically shaped narrative of the career of Jesus. Second, the historical study of Jesus should never have been seen as providing *the* single, unbiased record of Jesus of Nazareth; rather, such study will always result in more-or-less satisfactory accounts possessing both interpretive and historical force.

Practitioners of the Third Quest have tended to resist the hard-and-fast lines drawn and defended in earlier study of Jesus. As a Jew, Jesus must be seen within the diversity of Jewish beliefs and practices in the Second Temple period. As a teacher with disciples, Jesus must be seen as exercising a formative influence on the community that gathered around him and that continued after his crucifixion. As a Galilean, Jesus must have worked within (and against) the cultural realities of everyday experience; and his message must be understood more intimately within the social,

1.

The study of the historical Jesus has often been marred by sometimes even brazen attempts to recruit Jesus to one's own agenda, to remake him in our image. One of the most well-known scholars involved in this project has observed that study of the historical Jesus is an easy place to do autobiography and call it biography! Why do you suppose this is so?

economic, political, and religious realities of his world. From a practical standpoint, these considerations have given rise to the centrality of one question in the Third Quest: Why was Jesus crucified? Any interpretation of Jesus' career and claims that does not make sense of his execution on a Roman cross cannot be taken seriously, according to the Third Quest.

After more than two centuries of quests of the historical Jesus, what can be said? At the risk of oversimplifying what is at stake here, let me sketch two points. First, given the importance we place on God's acts within history, we may not downplay the implications of history for study of Jesus and the Gospels. Jesus was born in a particular time and place; this affirmation of our faith invites, even demands, that we grapple with the historical meaning of his message, as well as with its meaning in our own historical lives. On the other hand, what we as Christians regard as authoritative for Christian life and witness is not the Jesus given us by New Testament scholars but the Old and New Testaments as scriptural witness to the purpose of God in Christ. It is worth asking, therefore, what status any contemporary reconstruction of "the real human Jesus of Nazareth" might have. Must we accord privilege, even authoritative status, to the Jesus our historians, even our most able ones, are able to reconstruct? What of the Gospels that give witness to Jesus' life in its significance, the Old Testament that points to his coming, and the New Testament that takes as its fundamental point of departure the advent of the Messiah? Is it not these Scriptures that we expect to be proclaimed in our worship? Is it not these Scriptures to which we turn for enlightenment and direction as we seek to live faithfully before God?

"For This Reason I Came . . ."

The Gospels record a number of occasions in which Jesus announced the purpose of his coming. We might refer to these as "mission statements," and in the remainder of this chapter we will survey several of these representative declarations.

To Call Sinners

Early on in his ministry, according to the Gospel of Mark, Jesus extended the grace of discipleship to undesirable people:

> Jesus went out again beside the sea; the whole crowd gathered around him, and he taught them. As he was walking along, he saw Levi son of Alphaeus sitting at the toll booth, and he said to him, "Follow me." And he got up and followed him.
> And as he sat at dinner in Levi's house, many tax collectors and sinners were also sitting with Jesus and his disciples—for there were many who followed him. When the scribes of the Pharisees saw that he was eating with sinners and tax collectors, they said to his disciples, "Why does he eat with tax collectors and sinners?" When Jesus heard this, he said to them, "Those who are well have no need of a physician, but those who are sick; I have come to call not the righteous but sinners." (Mark 2:13-17)

These two paragraphs are held together by the common thread of Jesus crossing social and religious boundaries to include people who lived at the periphery of acceptable society in his circle of disciples and friends.

The force of this episode depends on our understanding three aspects of Jesus' social world. The first is the importance of meals. What one ate and with whom one ate—these questions had to do with the satiation of hunger, of course, but also signaled far-reaching messages in ancient Judaism. Table fellowship had to do with intimacy; to share a meal with others involved including them as extended family, so to speak. For many Jews, therefore, and especially for Pharisees, the table was the focus of issues of clean and unclean, acceptable and unacceptable. Second, among the range of possible occupations in first-century Palestine, collecting taxes was one of the least reputable. Tax collectors were the entrepreneurs of Roman antiquity, but they paid a heavy price for the wealth they were able to accumulate. This is because, among the social elite, what mattered was "old money" or "landed wealth"; those, like tax collectors, who had to earn their wealth, had no place in society's upper echelons. In popular opinion among Jews and other Romans, moreover, tax collectors were regarded as snoops, small-brained, and social drivel; one Roman writer placed them in the same category as pimps and traitors. For making sense of this passage, we must also come to terms with a third category: "sinners." In cases like these, "sinners" were not necessarily doers of great evil, nor were they simply people who failed to measure up to the requirements of the Jewish law. Rather, "sinner" had become in first-century Judaism a label to be placed on persons who failed to follow God in the way prescribed by one or another group within Judaism. That is, persons belonging to one Jewish group might refer to those of another group as "sinners," regarding them as little better than Gentiles.

Mark's portrait is a stark one, therefore. Little wonder that the legal experts questioned Jesus' behavior and attempted to influence his disciples to join them in censuring him. He extended table intimacy to society's "throwaways." Jesus had another perspective. He adopted the image of health care, portraying tax collectors and sinners as sick and himself as a physician. Crossing boundaries between the well and the sick—this is precisely what physicians do, and so Jesus was justified in his behavior. Jesus thus drew on traditional notions of the Lord as healer and of divine redemption as healing (for example, Exodus 15:26), where healing was defined as restoration to relationship with the Lord and his people—that is, as forgiveness. As "physician," Jesus crossed social and religious boundaries to open the way for spiritual and social restoration for society's outcasts.

To Seek and to Save the Lost

Luke includes the episode of the calling of Levi and the banquet that followed (Luke 5:27-32) but develops the importance of this presentation of Jesus even further by (1) portraying even more pervasively than Mark the hostility Jesus attracted on account of his table practices and partners at meal (for example, Luke 14; 15:1-2) and (2) telling the story of Zacchaeus (Luke 19:1-10), with its close parallels to the story of Levi. Both reveal the low status of tax collectors; both associate tax collectors with the label "sinner"; both indicate responses of discipleship (involving possessions and extending hospitality to Jesus); and both generalize from Jesus' encounter to summarize the nature of Jesus' mission: "I have come to call not the righteous but sinners to repentance" (Luke 5:32) and, "The Son of Man came to seek out and to save the lost" (19:10).

Zacchaeus is in some ways a strange character within the Gospel of Luke. He is introduced to us as wealthy and as a ruler (or chief) among tax collectors, and this in a Gospel narrative where the wealthy and rulers generally appear in opposition toward Jesus. He was also a tax collector and was regarded by the crowd as a sinner, and this in a Gospel where such persons habitually welcomed Jesus and were welcomed by him. By the end of the account, Jesus describes Zacchaeus as a "son of Abraham" (Luke 19:9), a status that was evidenced in Zacchaeus' behavior with his money: According to the Greek text, he gives half of what he has to the poor and makes fourfold restitution to any who are cheated under his watch (compare Luke 3:10-14). Additionally, Jesus regarded Zacchaeus as someone who had been "lost" but was now restored. From Luke's account, it is obvious that Zacchaeus was looked upon within his own community as an outsider; but Jesus restored him to his status among the people of God.

This is consistent with Jesus' mission and message throughout the Gospel of Luke. In Luke 4:18-19, Jesus announces that his mission is "to bring good news to the poor," a mission that is defined in three ways. First, it is a mission to "the poor"—who, in the Gospel of Luke, are identified above all as those who, for whatever reason, are marginalized in larger society. "Poor" is a large category of persons that includes the economically dispossessed, to be sure, but also those who are pushed to the periphery of their own communities on account of gender, family heritage, disease, religious purity, ethnicity, and so on. Second, Jesus' mission is one of "release"—which, in the Gospel of Luke, is developed in a variety of ways with regard to healing in all of its facets, or restoration to human wholeness. Third, in Jesus' sermon in Luke 4:16-30, he develops his mission in relation to the prophets Elijah and Elisha. Elijah, he points out, was sent by God to a woman, a non-Jew, a widow, while Elisha had been sent to a non-Jew whose disease, leprosy, symbolized his distance from Israel's God (see Leviticus 13–14). With reference to these examples, Jesus emphasizes that "good news to the poor" embraces the widow, the unclean, the Gentile, and all others whom society regards as misfits and outcasts—the least, the lost, and the left-out.

Taken together, these three statements of ministry (Luke 4:16-30; 5:27-32; 19:1-10) point to Jesus' mission as opening the way for the inclusion of people in God's kingdom who otherwise have no apparent claim on God. Within the social systems of the ancient Mediterranean world, they have been made outsiders. They belong to the class of "them." They are the poor to whom Jesus proclaims "good news," however; and this is key to the identity of his messianic mission.

To Serve and to Give His Life a Ransom for Many

The story is a familiar one. Jesus' disciples were arguing over the question, Who among them was the greatest? In this context, Jesus asserted, "The Son of Man came not to be served but to serve, and to give his life a ransom for many" (Matthew 20:28; Mark 10:45). This statement is often referred to as "the ransom saying," and it is crucial to our understanding of Jesus' mission.

In this narrative context, concerns with power grabbing and status seeking characteristic of the Roman Empire are on full display. The world under Caesar Augustus was unified not only by one emperor but also by a political order based on the ethics of patronage. Augustus assumed for himself the role of benefactor or patron for all of the Roman world. In doing so, he adopted a role that was formalized in the culture of the Mediterranean: Patrons gave gifts to their clients, and clients owed allegiance and honor to their patrons. Slaves were indebted to their masters. Sons were under the rule of their fathers. Clients were bound to their patrons and often had clients of their own. Spun like a web throughout the Empire, these lines of obligation left people in never-ending cycles of obligation to others.

Against such a world order, Jesus' message stands in stark contrast. For example, Jesus' disciples are said repeatedly to have struggled with the question of who among them was the greatest. Jesus' response was to reject such maneuvering outright and to assert that the kingdom of God belonged to little children. He further insisted that status in the community be measured by one's role as a servant. Service, of course, was expected when relating to people of higher status; but Jesus, even while acknowledging his own superior status when measured in the company of his followers, communicated by word and deed that service was to be given to those of lower status, including (or especially) little children.

Jesus further undermined the ethics of obligation by insisting that people give without expectation of return. Within the normal social roles, gifts brought with them expectations of reciprocity. Jesus set forth for his listeners an alternative way of life, not run by relations of debt and obligation. The household he imagined was one in which people would be treated as family, with services performed and goods shared without the attachment of reciprocal obligation. As Jesus summarized, "Love your enemies, do good, and lend, expecting nothing in return" (Luke 6:35). What is more, Jesus rooted this subversive ethic in the human vocation to imitate God: "Be merciful, just as your Father is merciful" (Luke 6:36).

In this way, Jesus opposed the Roman order at the most fundamental of levels, replacing a culture of debt and obligation with a form of life that took as its point of beginning the generosity of God, the merciful Father who extends grace even to the ungrateful and the wicked.

The episode recounted in Mark 10:35-45, sketched briefly above, indicates how pervasive "politics as usual" would have been, even to the point of infiltrating the inner circle of Jesus' disciples. Those who follow Jesus are not immune to the struggle for power and quest for status as measured by the standards of public opinion. Here Mark features a bid for recognition and honor in the form of requests for the two primary seats of honor, on either side of the host in the kingdom banquet, for James and John. The anger of the other followers of Jesus on hearing of this surreptitious bid for distinction was likewise rooted in the ancient, competitive game of status seeking. If James and John were granted the highest positions, what rank would be left for the others?

These qualities and the behaviors they sponsored surface throughout the Gospels; and Jesus consistently censured them—for example, when he gave advice on dinner invitations and seating arrangements (Luke 14:7-24) and when he urged hospitality to the least impressive inhabitants of the Roman social world, little children (see Mark 9:33-37; 10:13-16). In the ransom saying, Jesus toppled status-seeking practices.

Jesus illustrated his teaching with reference to his own mission. Consequently, the ransom saying functions both as an example that confirmed the ethic he had just proposed and as Jesus' self-disclosure of the life goal given him by God. The climax of his mission, the reason for his having "come," was this: "to give his life [as] a ransom for many" (Mark 10:45). "Ransom" invites reflection on two images. One was borrowed from the Roman slave trade, where a ransom might serve as the price of emancipation, after which the one freed belonged to the one who paid the price. The second is of even greater importance and derives from Israel's own past; God "ransomed" Israel, delivering the people from slavery in Egypt (Exodus 6:6; 15:13). Jesus both instructs his followers to devote their lives to the service of others and reveals at the same time the purpose of his own life, even to the point that he will embrace death on behalf of others.

The Challenge to Be God's People

I have elaborated only three "mission statements" that help to define the substance of the messianic mission. Others might have been developed as well—for example, Jesus' relationship to the law of Moses ("I have come not to

2.

In the final decade of the twentieth century, millions of Americans purchased and wore bracelets, shirts, and other clothing embossed with the initials "WWJD": "What Would Jesus Do?" As you think about Jesus' mission as reflected in the purpose statements we have discussed, how would you answer the question, WWJD?

abolish but to fulfill" [Matthew 5:17].) or his campaign to bring life ("I came that they may have life, and have it abundantly" [John 10:10; see John 3:16; 12:47].). What is already clear, however, is (1) the high degree to which Jesus' ministry was purposeful and (2) how his ministry pointed beyond itself to God's graciousness in and judgment on the world.

Naturally, Jesus' message was oriented toward the first-century Roman world and thus was in part determined by that world. He addressed issues that were pressing in his own day. He was hardly a captive of the social systems of his world, however. In fact, in the examples we have discussed, more often than not, Jesus exploited the conventions and commitments of those around him in order to drive home an alternative vision of God and to call for new definitions of fidelity to God. For example, he did not deny that table fellowship signaled kinship and intimacy; rather, he capitalized on the significance of table fellowship by embracing social and spiritual outsiders as though they were members of his extended family. At other times, his message is even more direct in the challenges it presents. In the face of widespread tendencies toward status seeking and the exploitation of others by means of relationships governed by debt, he called for and modeled ways of life in which human interactions are not governed by boundary keeping, the power of reciprocity, or the constant measuring of one's relative honor. Jesus' ministry called others to see the world differently and to act accordingly.

To put it somewhat differently, throughout his life, Jesus oriented his mission toward summoning the people of God *to be the people of God.* The messianic mission had as its ultimate aim the restoration of Israel, but this entailed calling Israel to its true self and forming a community that would embody within itself God's character and God's purpose. The mission statements we have discussed are important precisely because they indicate how Jesus was able to sketch and enact a vision of the world, or rather a vision of what the world is to be, that ran counter to the universe administered by Rome and embraced by the Jewish leadership in Jerusalem. Understood in this light, the appropriate

3

One of the remarkable aspects of Jesus' ministry was his capacity to challenge widespread assumptions about "the way the world is" by proclaiming an alternative world and acting as though that new world were already in place. In what ways does your church model Jesus' ministry at this point?

response for the people of God was and continues to be repentance.

The reality of Jesus' mission may seem paradoxical. Titles like "Son of God," "Messiah," and "Lord" reveal Jesus as unique in his relationship to God, a person with a special purpose and a singular capacity to make available God's gifts of salvation. We might be forgiven for thinking that the immediate implication of the Incarnation is that Jesus somehow lived "above it all," removed from society's dregs, actively engaged in meaningful discourse with the nobility of his day. In actuality, however, the mission of the Messiah is represented at its most profound and characteristic when Jesus took the little children into his arms or held the arms of the leper. Does this mean that the wealthy and famous are thereby excluded from his ministry? Of course not!— That is, provided they are willing to receive the healing ministry of Jesus at their own points of need and to join with him in sharing good news among the marginal of the world.

6

Why Did Jesus Have to Die?

Key Concepts:
- What are the primary lines of evidence for the historical certainty of Jesus' crucifixion under Pontius Pilate?
- What is the significance of Jesus' ministry of healing? How might his healing activity be related to the manner of his death?
- In what way might Jesus' proclamation about the importance of little children in the kingdom of God have threatened the Roman Empire?
- What did Jesus do to merit execution on a Roman cross as a political risk?

Were you there when they crucified my Lord?
Were you there when they crucified my Lord?
Oh! sometimes it causes me to tremble, tremble, tremble.
Were you there when they crucified my Lord?[1]

The words of this African American spiritual are almost unique in our hymnals. True, there are many hymns, songs, and anthems that tell of Jesus' crucifixion. Few address the mystery and horror of the cross of Christ in the way this one does, however. Indeed, "sometimes" when I reflect on the cross, "it causes me to tremble, tremble, tremble."

For many of us, our typical response to the cross is represented in other hymns, with words that interpret the cross theologically, in light of its benefits for us. That is, our interpretations of the cross have tended to see the Crucifixion as the starting point for our life before God. Only thus can we sing with Isaac Watts,

> When I survey the wondrous cross
> on which the Prince of Glory died,
> my richest gain I count but loss,
> and pour contempt on all my pride.[2]

Without in any way downplaying the significance of the death of Jesus for our salvation (on which we will focus in Chapter 7), in order to understand the work of Christ, it is also important to examine the cross from another perspective. Our concern in this chapter is the historical problem of the crucifixion of Jesus. Sharply put, the problem is this: What did Jesus do to merit execution on a Roman cross, that is, to be condemned to this heinous form of capital punishment as a threat to the Roman Empire?

The Crucifixion of Jesus in History

With regard to the historical evidence for Jesus, nothing is more certain about his life than his death. The Apostles' Creed reads, "suffered under Pontius Pilate, crucified, dead, and buried." Here is a profound affirmation of the depth of the Incarnation:

> Being found in human form,
> he humbled himself
> and became obedient to the
> point of death—
> even death on a cross.
> (Philippians 2:7-8)

This event is recounted in extraordinary detail in the Passion narratives of the New Testament Gospels. In fact, among the evidence for crucifixion in the ancient world, the Gospels provide the most dramatic representation of the act of crucifixion available to us. In addition, the execution of Jesus by crucifixion is mentioned repeatedly as a historical event in other New Testament writings. Outside of Christian writings, Jesus' death under Pilate's authority is also mentioned by two historians of this period: Josephus and Tacitus.

The text from Josephus is found in his history of the Jewish people and reads as follows:

> About this time there lived Jesus, a wise man, if indeed one ought to call him a human. For he was one who performed miracles and was a teacher of such people as accept the truth gladly. He won over many Jews and many of the Greeks. He was the Messiah. When Pilate, upon hearing him accused by the people of the highest standing among us, had condemned him to be crucified, those who had in the first place come to love him did not give up their affection for him.[3]

Josephus was no follower of Jesus, so some parts of this text have caused scholars to question whether Josephus could have written the whole of it. In particular, the unabashed affirmation of Jesus' messiahship is suspect. Many now believe that the original form of Josephus' *Antiquities of the Jews* did contain some statement regarding Jesus that was later altered by Christian scribes. That original text would have included reference to Jesus' teaching and his reputation as a worker of powerful deeds, as well as his crucifixion. In his *Annals* (written shortly after A.D. 115), the Roman historian Tacitus briefly mentions the persecution of the Christians at Rome in A.D. 64. The relevant passage appears after Tacitus mentions suspicions that Nero had started the great fire that damaged Rome: "To dispel the rumor, Nero substituted as culprits, and treated with the most extreme punishments, some people, popularly called Christians, whose disgraceful activities were notorious. The originator of that name, Christus, had been executed when Tiberius was emperor by the order of the procurator Pontius Pilate."[4]

In addition to these instances of direct attestation among non-Christian sources, a further piece of evidence underscores the historicity of Jesus' crucifixion. This is the offense of the abhorrent death of Jesus that opponents of the Christian message seized upon in order to discredit the claims made by Christians on behalf of Jesus. Justin Martyr wrote, "They say that our madness consists in the fact that we put a crucified man in second place after the unchangeable and eternal God, the creator of the world."[5]

If the *fact* that Jesus was crucified under Roman rule is secure, what does this tell us about the *nature* of Jesus' death? In spite of popular dramatizations of ancient crucifixion in sermons and books today, we actually know very little about the techniques used in crucifixion. The Gospels themselves report only that "they crucified him" (Mark 15:24; Luke 23:33; John 19:18), without describing how this took place. Victims might have been fixed to a stake or tree in order to die or only after death. They might have been bound or nailed to the cross. People condemned to execution in this manner might have been affixed to the wood in any position imaginable. In conducting the act of crucifixion itself, Roman soldiers apparently followed no instruction manual.

Other aspects of crucifixion are clearer, of which two are especially important: (1) Crucifixion was not the most painful way to execute someone in antiquity, but it proved to be the most abhorrent. This was partially a result of the public humiliation that accompanied the act. Bound or nailed to a stake, tree, or cross, the victim faced death with all organs intact and with little blood loss. Death usually came slowly, perhaps over several days, as the body surrendered to shock. Humiliation was increased by the general policy of denying the victim a proper burial but instead leaving the decaying corpse on the cross or tree as carrion for the birds. (2) Crucifixion was reserved by the Romans for those who resisted the authority of Roman occupation. Crucifixion was thus used as a deterrent. The place of execution was invariably a well-traveled road or crossroads so the general population would be given a somber reminder of the fate of those who dared to engage in sedition against the Roman Empire.

1.

Have you ever imagined Jesus as a "political risk"? How does the historical fact of his execution as a dissident reshape your previous understandings of him?

Jesus: A Political Risk?

Why was Jesus put to death? The easy answer to this question is that Jesus was regarded as a political risk and was found guilty of sedition. But how could this have been? What prompted this view of Jesus? Undoubtedly, diverse motives were at work in the decision to condemn Jesus to a rebel's death. For the Jewish elite in Jerusalem, Jesus had to die because he appeared to be a religious deceiver and false prophet who must be purged from the community of the people of Israel, lest he lead them away from the Lord God. From the perspective of Pilate, Rome's representative, the problem must have lain elsewhere. The death of Jesus must have been intended to serve the purpose of deterrence, demonstrating for all to see the fate of those with pretensions to the throne or whose actions might incite mob action against the Roman state.

In order to understand better the threat Jesus might have posed, we should remind ourselves of one of the fundamental realities of life in the Roman world. For American Christians today, it is easy to practice a kind of religious faith that belongs to the private sphere of our lives. We may attend church, even nurture a private devotional life; but we are often expected to leave our faith at home when we move into the public sphere. Unfortunately, this is the direction in which the First Amendment, guaranteeing the separation of church and state, has been interpreted in our time. Such ways of thinking were simply unavailable in the first-century world. Institutions like the Roman Empire or the Jewish Temple were the points of intersection for all of life: religion, economics, politics, and so on. Private and public did not exist as categories. Religion was not a category separate from negotiating for food in the marketplace. In fact, institutions typically came to believe and to perpetuate the belief that they existed because they were created and maintained by God. In such a world, a "political" violation was by definition religious; and a religious transgression was political. Such violations upset the moral order; they disturbed the "divinely ordained" distribution of power and wealth. They presented an alternative under-standing of the world and, therefore, of God.

Before moving on to further discussion of Jesus the polit-ical risk, let me try to illustrate what is at stake here. One of my earliest recollections of the church down the street from our own was the way they conducted their business meetings. Into the wee hours of the night, members of the church would sit in the sanctuary arguing over matters such as whether to purchase brass offering plates or silver ones. As a pastor, I remember the hostility I invited when I moved the communal recitation of the Lord's Prayer from its place in the worship service after the Opening Prayer to a new location after the Pastoral Prayer. And today the sto-ries of conflict over worship styles, old and new songs, organs and guitars, are legion. Why do we care so deeply about these issues? Would we struggle with each other so desperately if these were mere matters of personal prefer-ence? In reality, we tend to think that "the way I see things is the way things really are"; that "others should thus see things in the same way I do"; and, indeed, that "the way I see things is the way God made them to be." Hence, our debates are often not about the relative merits of brass or silver in worship paraphernalia, for example. They run much deeper. We believe at some basic level that they have to do with who God is and how God has made things to be.

If this is true for us, it was much truer in Roman antiq-uity where people did not tend to catalog different aspects of life into separate categories but where all of life was per-meated by the will of the gods or the will of God.

Jesus, Worker of Miracles

According to the Gospel of Luke, Jesus was indicted by the Jewish leaders before Pilate for "perverting our nation, forbidding us to pay taxes to the emperor, and saying that he himself is the Messiah. . . . He stirs up the people by teaching throughout all Judea" (Luke 23:1-5). This does not mean that the Jewish people were responsible for Jesus'

2,

Reflect on the reality that the Jewish leadership in Jerusalem joined the Romans in opposing Jesus. What does this suggest about the extent to which the leading institutions and personnel had grown comfortable with "the Roman way"? How easy is it for the church today to disentangle itself from its wider culture in order to have a prophetic ministry?

execution, but it does suggest the important role of the Jewish elite in Jerusalem in opposing Jesus. In a significant sense, Jesus and the Jewish leadership were struggling with each other over what it meant to be faithful to the God of Israel, and thus over who would lead the Jewish people faithfully. Indeed, the political substance of the accusation Luke records was clearly directed at piquing the interest of the Roman governor. More interesting for us at this point, however, is the language of "perverting our nation" and "stir[ring] up the people." This is because Deuteronomy 13 warns of persons who would come, false prophets who would lead the people away from the ways of God by wondrous works. Jesus, it would appear, was branded a false prophet who therefore deserved the death penalty.

Interestingly, Jewish tradition from the second and third centuries A.D. provides evidence of the same charge. One Jewish text refers to Jesus as one who "practiced sorcery and enticed and led Israel astray,"[6] while another says of "Jesus the Nazarene" that he "practiced magic and led Israel astray."[7] Similarly in the second century, the Christian apologist Justin Martyr argued against a Jewish view that Jesus was a "magician and deceiver of God's people."[8] This proliferation of evidence strongly supports the view that (1) Jesus was known as a miracle worker, (2) his miraculous activity was seen as a diabolic means for leading Israel away from their God, and (3) he was thus identified as a false prophet who deserved the death penalty.

Clearly, the presence of the miraculous in the ministry of Jesus was a key factor, so much so that it will be prudent to examine the portrait of Jesus as a healer and miracle worker in more detail. This will help us to situate the nature of his ministry historically, to understand better its importance, and to grasp how miracle working could have brought Jesus into hostile encounters with the Jewish leadership.

Elsewhere in Luke's narrative, Peter summarizes the ministry of Jesus: Having been anointed by God with the Holy Spirit and power, Jesus "went about doing good and healing all who were oppressed by the devil" (Acts 10:38). A perusal of the Gospels, especially the first three, will indicate how thoroughly the miraculous pervaded the ministry of Jesus. In the Gospel of Matthew alone, we find nineteen stories of the miraculous alongside four summary statements indicating healing as a distinctive property of Jesus' activity. Mark records eighteen miracle stories and four summaries, and Luke has twenty stories and three summaries. Of course, these Gospels occasionally report the same episode; but the list of independent accounts is still impressive: six episodes of exorcism, seventeen accounts of healing, and eight "nature miracles." In addition, the Evangelists allude to miracles that are not specifically recounted; Jesus interprets the significance of his healing ministry; and his opponents offer alternative interpretations of Jesus' miracles. Added to this are the "signs" performed by Jesus in the Gospel of John and the witness to Jesus' powerful deeds by the first-century Jewish historian Josephus (see above). The conclusion is inescapable that healing was essential to Jesus' ministry.

In terms of the criteria of authenticity mentioned in the previous chapter, support from the criterion of multiple attestation is obvious. What of the criterion of dissimilarity? We may recall that this criterion allows one to judge as authentic only those traditions attributed to Jesus that cannot be said to have been introduced by means of Jewish or Christian influence. What about other healers in the wider world of first-century antiquity and within the Christian communities after Jesus?

Within Jewish circles, two candidates are sometimes compared with Jesus: Honi the Circle-Drawer and Hanina ben Dosa. We also know of Apollonius of Tyana, a first-century Gentile miracle worker. Traditions surrounding these persons are important both for indicating that healers were not unknown (or simply dismissed as charlatans) in the world of Jesus and also for demonstrating how Jesus was dissimilar from such potential analogues as these. Both Honi the Circle-Drawer and Hanina ben Dosa easily qualify as "holy men," but neither can be called a "miracle worker" with respect to their *characteristic* activity. What is more, these two persons were known for their calling on Yahweh to work in spectacular ways. Jesus, on the other hand, is distinguished by his *typical* behavior as a healer and, more importantly, is portrayed as one who exercised in a direct way the saving power of God. He did not ask God to intervene on behalf of those in need of a miracle but pronounced their healing directly in "speech-acts" that assumed his possession of divine authority to do so.

These speech-acts also distinguish the healing of Jesus from that of his disciples, at least as this is evidenced in the Acts of the Apostles. The disciples did not assume direct access to divine power even when they were engaged in ministries of signs and wonders; indeed, they often recoiled from the suggestion of others that they possessed divine power (for example, Acts 14:14-15) and instead pronounced healing "in the name of Jesus" (for example, Acts 3:6, 16). Unlike Apollonius, Jesus often emphasized the component of faith in his ministry of healing—so much so that, according to the Gospels, one of the characteristic assertions of Jesus was, "Your faith has made you well." Jesus, then, was both like and unlike other healers; and the portrait of Jesus as healer satisfies the criterion of dissimilarity.

What of the significance of Jesus' healing? Two responses suggest themselves. First, Jesus' healing is a sign of the in-breaking kingdom of God. Isaiah 35:1-7 promises the coming of God in history to bring salvation and judgment, promising, among other things, "the eyes of the blind shall be opened, / and the ears of the deaf unstopped." Similarly, in its Greek version, Isaiah 61:1-2 anticipates the coming of the eschaton as a time when the blind will receive their sight. The relevance of this Isaianic vision rests on the implicit and explicit use of that vision by the Evangelists to indicate the significance of Jesus' ministry as a healer. Mark 7:37, for example, records how the crowds were astonished by a miracle of healing and responded in words echoing Isaiah 35:5-6: "He even makes the deaf to hear and the mute to speak." Matthew 11:2-5 and Luke 7:18-22 (see Luke 4:18-19) recall in an explicit way the language and eschatological vision of Isaiah and in doing so serve to communicate (1) that Jesus is God's Anointed One and (2) that with Jesus' advent the new creation that fulfills the prophecies of Isaiah is unfolding. Jesus' perspective in Luke 11:20, though not tied into Isaianic expectations, is nevertheless comparable: "If it is by the finger of God that I cast out the demons, then the kingdom of God has come to you."

The healing activity of Jesus thus pointed beyond itself to the nature of the times, to the new era being introduced in Jesus' coming. God's redemptive purpose was breaking into the world; the kingdom of God was already making its presence felt.

Second, Jesus' ministry of healing speaks to our understanding of "health" and human wholeness. It is worth reflecting on the reality that, in the Greco-Roman world, *savior* and *salvation* were words the meaning of which overlapped considerably with the terms *healer/physician* and *healing/health*. This is pertinent because it suggests immediately how fuzzy would have been the lines we so easily draw today between "spiritual health," "emotional health," and "physical health." A close examination of the healing episodes recounted by the Gospel writers will quickly indicate how rarely "physical healing" was at center stage. In comparison with notions of "healing and health" in the Gospels, ours is an overly constricted view of health, since it does not account very well for either the human being in his or her social relations or the entanglement of human existence in cosmic disorder. In Jesus' ministry we discover a far more integrated perspective with regard to who human beings are within themselves and in relation to each other with reference to the vision of salvation and new creation propagated by Jesus in his healing ministry.

For both these reasons, we are apt to miss the importance of Jesus' healing ministry. This is because we tend to see its significance in the miraculous character of the events of healing and marvel at these manifestations of supernatural power. Their real importance lies elsewhere, in their witness to the reality that, in the presence of Jesus, the era of salvation had arrived, enabling people to live life again as God has purposed life to be lived.

This brief discussion of Jesus' healing ministry reveals two important and closely related affirmations. First, Jesus' healing was pivotal to the meaning of his ministry; and, second, his healing ministry was capable of more than one interpretation. For the New Testament, Jesus is the authorized agent of Yahweh's healing beneficence, the presence of which signals in Jesus' ministry the presence of God's end-time rule. For the Jewish leaders in Jerusalem, Jesus' healing activity marked him as a false prophet who manipulated God's people and subverted God's way and therefore was deserving of death.

Jesus and Roman Peace

Perhaps the most sacred aspect of Roman life was the well-known *pax romana,* the peace of Rome. The easiest way to run afoul of Rome was to question that peace; indeed, the primary purpose of the Roman presence in Palestine in the first century was not to extend Rome's borders farther but simply to keep the peace. The Jewish council bore authentic witness to first-century realities in John 11:47-48 when they expressed their fear of an uprising that would cause Rome to come and destroy both the Temple and the Jewish nation.

Not surprisingly, then, the religion of Rome, though pluralistic in many ways, was manifestly a religion of legitimation of the existing social order. One way to grasp this aspect of Roman life is to recall the centrality of the ethics of patronage to the Roman Empire. Rome was unified not only by one emperor but also by a political order based on patronage. Augustus assumed for himself the role of benefactor or patron for all of the Roman world. In doing so, he adopted a role that was formalized as one of the most prominent and taken-for-granted ingredients of life throughout the Empire. What we need to add to our earlier comments is that even the emperor had client status of a sort, for the hierarchy of patronal relations extended beyond the human sphere to include the gods. Although he was not himself divine, the emperor was the recipient of the gods' patronage and served as their special agent. Thus, the reciprocity of patronal relations that obligated slaves to masters, sons to fathers, the elite to the emperor, was an extension of the emperor's (and with him, all of Rome's) indebtedness to the gods. The honor due the elite of the city and the allegiance due the emperor and his representatives throughout the Empire—these obligations were divinely ordained. And the political order (and with it, one's place in that hierarchy) found its legitimation in the gods themselves. It was sacred.

Jesus did indeed subvert this world order, rejecting all posturing for honor and recognition. Moreover, in a profound inversion of the accepted world order, he asserted that the kingdom of God belonged to little children and to those who treated little children with the honor one would normally allocate to nobility. "Welcome" children, he said; that is, extend hospitality and honor to those who occupied the bottom rung of society's ladder of respect and recognition (for example, Mark 9:33-37). Jesus' message thus crossed the grain of the Roman political order not only at the level of practices and attitudes but also with respect to the most basic questions about "how the world works."

Working against the social system of the Empire involved Jesus in a religious infraction, for the social system was authorized by the gods. Jesus thus ran afoul of the religious-political order of the Roman world and taught others to do the same. Therefore, he must have been regarded as a political risk.

The political threat Jesus posed to the Roman world can be developed along additional lines as well. His prophetic action in the Temple, during which he upset normal Temple functions, would have attracted the attention of those concerned most basically with maintaining the status quo. The crowds that gathered around Jesus when he entered into Jerusalem and during his ministry of teaching in the Temple would also have attracted Roman attention.

Against the backdrop of the religious importance of Roman peace, it thus begins to make sense that Jesus was a political risk. His message proposed a topsy-turvy construction of the world in which salvation was not tied to the success of the emperor, and honor was not related to one's position on the social hierarchy.

Jesus, Messiah, Revolutionary

Though we have no evidence to suggest that Jesus claimed for himself the title "King of the Jews," it was under such a placard that he was crucified (see, for exam-

3.

Have you ever suffered for maintaining a position in which you believed strongly? How did those around you respond to your decision to hold fast and accept the consequences of your convictions?

ple, Mark 15:26). Of course, Jesus' followers would have found the charges brought against him ironic; crucified as a messianic pretender, he was recognized by them as truly being the Messiah.

Measured in light of the nature of the charges brought against him, the political risk associated with Jesus is understandable. What we must grasp is that, in the end, the charges brought against Jesus were neither trumped up nor artificial. Rather, they spoke to what was indeed revolutionary about Jesus' message; and they show that Jesus went to his death on account of issues that grew out of the center of his mission. Following the purpose of God with radical obedience meant for Jesus that he attracted the hostility of too many people who read the purpose of God (or the gods) differently. In the end, Jesus had to die because too many people, both Jewish and Roman leaders, opposed him and his ministry.

[1] From "Were You There," in *The United Methodist Hymnal* (Copyright © 1989 The United Methodist Publishing House); 288.

[2] From "When I Survey the Wondrous Cross," in *The United Methodist Hymnal*; 298.

[3] From *Jewish Antiquities,* by Josephus; 18.3.3.

[4] From *The Annals,* by Tacitus; 15.44.

[5] From *First Apology,* by Justin Martyr; 13.4.

[6] From *Sanhedrin* 43a of the Babylonian Talmud.

[7] From *Sanhedrin* 107b of the Babylonian Talmud.

[8] From *Dialogue,* by Justin Martyr; 7.3.

7

The Mystery of the Cross

Key Concepts:
- What paths did early Christians take in order to articulate a positive understanding of Jesus' crucifixion?
- In the history of the church, what have been the three most prominent ways of describing the Atonement?
- Why is there no one, single way of developing the theological significance of the death of Christ in the New Testament?
- What does it mean to speak of the "wrath of God" in Paul's writings? How is this related to God's love?
- What four biblical themes are crucial for our thinking about the meaning of Jesus' death?

The enigma of the crucified Christ is nowhere better portrayed than in the last chapter of Luke's Gospel. On the Sunday after Jesus' horrible death, two of his disciples are returning to their home in Emmaus—according to Luke, about seven miles from Jerusalem. As we pick up the story, Jesus has joined these travelers, though they do not recognize him.

"What are you discussing with each other while you walk along?" [he inquired.] . . . Cleopas answered him, "Are you the only stranger in Jerusalem who does not know the things that have taken place there in these days?" He asked them, "What things?" They replied, "The things about

Jesus of Nazareth, who was a prophet mighty in deed and word before God and all the people, and how our chief priests and leaders delivered him up to be condemned to death and crucified him. But we had hoped that he was the one to redeem Israel." (Luke 24:17-21)

Their hopes were dashed by the Crucifixion. From their vantage point, Jesus' execution on a Roman cross disqualified him from being "the one to redeem Israel."

These Emmaus disciples should not be too readily faulted for their lack of understanding. After all, according to views current in the first century, people who were crucified suffered humiliation of the most extreme kind; and among the Jews, victims of crucifixion were believed to bear the curse of God as well. This was because contemporary interpretation understood Deuteronomy 21:22-23—"anyone hung on a tree"—with reference to the act of crucifixion (compare Acts 5:30: 10:39; 13:29; Galatians 3:13-14). How could one who had been cursed by God (that is, a victim of crucifixion) be God's Anointed One (that is, the Messiah)? Is this not a contradiction in terms? The path to a positive understanding of Jesus' crucifixion could not have been self-evident.

Two things are nonetheless obvious in earliest Christian testimony. First, Christians did not attempt to sweep the problem of the cross under the rug so as to hide it from view. From earliest times, and in myriad ways, they searched the Scriptures of Israel for insight into the meaning of what must have seemed to them at first to be an irreconcilable tragedy. Second, then, Christians were never content merely to speak of the historical event of the cross. Thus, in the early creedal statement cited by Paul in 1 Corinthians 15:3-5, we do not read, "Jesus died on a cross" but rather, "Christ died for our sins in accordance with the scriptures." The first statement is accurate, of course; but it has no particular relevance. Many thousands of people were crucified under the Romans; why bother to mention one in particular? What bearing might it have on history? At the most, it might have been remembered anecdotally as an illustration of troubled Roman-Jewish relations in the first third of the first century A.D. "Christ died for our sins" is an affirmation of an altogether different sort, one that gave a profound depth of meaning to the death of Jesus for those first Christians and, indeed, for the whole world then and since.

Our focus in this chapter is to explore that depth of meaning. Specifically, we are interested here in the doctrine of the Atonement, which addresses the question, What is the saving significance of Jesus' death? Many models for making sense of the Atonement have been offered during the first two millennia of the history of Christianity. My plan is to discuss the three most prominent of these before turning more explicitly to sample briefly some of the ways in which the New Testament itself addresses this question.

Classical Models of the Atonement

In the first centuries of the life of the church, reflection on the *person* of Jesus coalesced around affirmations of the pre-existence and deity of Jesus. Classical faith thus affirms the doctrine of the Incarnation, even as it struggles to represent the mystery of how Jesus is fully human and fully divine. No such accord has ever existed with regard to the Atonement. Instead, not only in Scripture, but throughout the history of the church's faith and mission, the significance of Jesus' death has been articulated in different ways at different times in different places. *That* God took on human form in Christ Jesus is secure. To paraphrase Anselm, *why* God embraced the human condition so fully as to suffer an ignominious death is a question that begs for interpretation and that can never be exhausted.

Why the church has never been content with a single interpretation of Jesus' death is clear. If communicating the good news is like good journalism, then we can appreciate the need to address particular audiences mindful of what that audience can and will take for granted. Seen in this light, talk about God, and in this case about the work of Christ, must take seriously the cultural contexts (whether in a seminar at church, at an inner-city mission, or on the streets of Bangladesh) in which we hope to gain a hearing.

How is the death of Jesus "for us"? Numerous models have been proposed—for example, governmental, satisfaction, moral influence, dramatic, incarnational, ransom, substitution, and more. Three have been especially prominent, however.

The Model of Satisfaction

Formulated by Anselm of Canterbury (1033–1109), the model of satisfaction was first proposed as an alternative to an earlier "ransom theory," which had it that the death of Jesus "ransomed" sinful humanity away from the grip of the devil. Anselm saw that the fundamental problem with salvation was not concerned with the devil or with any "right" or "authority" of the devil over human lives. Rather, the problem of salvation had to do with the wrong done to God. Although humans were created for and called to faithfulness and service, they have instead chosen the way of rebellion and pride.

In his attempt to communicate the meaning of the Atonement for people in his day, Anselm reflected on the feudal system of his world, in which a lord and his vassals lived in peace when both fulfilled their obligations. Lords provided capital and protection. Vassals provided loyalty and tribute. In this world, the social order depended on proper honor and service being given to one's lord. Anselm thus portrayed God as a feudal lord, whose honor had been challenged by the behavior of his vassals, the human race. God therefore required satisfaction, a settlement, before humanity could be forgiven and brought back into peace with God.

For Anselm, the dilemma was this. As the infraction originated with humans, so reparations must be made from the human side of the social equation. Yet, on account of the magnitude of the violation, only God would be capable of making amends. Anselm asked, "Why did God become human?" and answered that, without the Incarnation, redemption would be impossible. Only Christ, divine and human, could live the faithful life required of all humanity and so in his death satisfy God's sense of justice and honor.

In more recent years, Anselm's model has been detached from the cultural context in which he developed it and relocated in the American justice system. In our criminal justice system, "satisfaction" has to do with the apprehension and punishment of the guilty, while for Anselm and his contemporaries, satisfaction hinged on the fulfillment of certain obligations related to loyalty and honor. Consequently, Anselm's categories of honor and shame have been replaced with our categories of guilt and innocence, with the result that we have developed a quite different model, usually called "penal substitutionary atonement." According to this model, because we are guilty, we must be punished. Jesus, however, took upon himself the punishment due us so that God might respond to us with love rather than with anger. This is a good illustration of how models of the Atonement develop, but it also illustrates how they must be measured in light of the biblical witness to the work of Christ. As we will see shortly, the model of penal substitutionary atonement is based in views of God and Christ that are hard to square with Scripture.

The Model of Exemplary Love

Peter Abelard (1079–1142) joined Anselm in taking issue with a "ransom" theory of the Atonement based on what was "due" the devil, but he was not impressed with the idea of "satisfaction" either. For Abelard the focus lay not in making reparations toward God, but in the consequences of reconciliation in the commitments and behaviors of the human being. The Atonement, then, was the decisive disclosure of the love of God, which in turn enables and calls forth dispositions and behaviors of love from humanity. Sometimes referred to as a theory of "moral influence," Abelard's model of the Atonement emphasized moral freedom for responsive love.

The Model of Conquest

Drawing on the earlier views of Irenaeus (*ca* A.D. 130–202) and Luther (1483–1546), Gustaf Aulén in the twentieth century reinvigorated the Atonement as the conquest of the rule of Satan. The cross of Christ is thus the decisive moment in the cosmic drama in which good and evil war against each other. In the cross, evil is defeated

1.

In the last two hundred years, talk about the saving significance of the cross has often been tied to images of divine retribution and God's anger against humanity. How have these images shaped the life and message of the church? What would happen if our understanding of the message of the cross was guided less by God's working against human rebellion and more by God's working for human restoration?

and forfeits its power over humanity and, indeed, over the whole cosmos. God is revealed as victorious, and the world is reconciled to God.

Again, other models of the Atonement have been championed throughout the history of Christianity. The importance of these three does not lie necessarily in their greater faithfulness to Scripture but rather in their capacity to address particular historical moments with the inexhaustible wealth of the meaning of Jesus' death. Christians involved in mission in their own neighborhoods and throughout the world may be drawn to these models for their relevance or for their usefulness as conversation partners in the ongoing task of communicating the saving significance of Jesus' death.

The Atonement and the New Testament

The variety of models for making sense of the saving significance of Jesus' death on display in the history of the church has deep roots in the New Testament. In the Scriptures we find a virtual smorgasbord of ways to understand the meaning and relevance of Jesus' death. This is because of (1) the need to address the significance of the cross to particular needs in the Christian mission and in Christian communities and because of (2) the fact that the death of Jesus is an event of such pivotal importance to the plan of God that its relevance is immeasurable.

Let me give one example from the pages of the New Testament of how interpretations of the cross can be context specific. One of Paul's challenges as he wrote Second Corinthians was the nature of his own relationship to the Christians at Corinth—a relationship that had developed into one of discord. Thus, when Paul began to articulate the significance of Christ's death in 2 Corinthians 5, we may not be surprised to discover that he employed the language of reconciliation. The Christian message, he insisted, is "the message of reconciliation" (5:19). Paul had been entrusted with the ministry of reconciliation; and the gospel call is, "Be reconciled!" Thus, in the context of one of his most elegant summaries of the work of Christ ("In

Christ God was reconciling the world to himself" [5:19].), he can plead, "Our heart is wide open to you. There is no restriction in our affections, but only in yours. In return . . . open wide your hearts also" (2 Corinthians 6:11-13).

Reconciliation is not the only way Paul expressed the meaning of Jesus' death. In fact, Paul used this term only rarely in his letters. His decision to employ it here undoubtedly grew out of the particular needs he faced as he wrote to the Corinthians.

Looking at Paul's letters as a whole, we may with good reason get the impression that Paul never tired of adding new images to his vocabulary for communicating the saving importance of the cross. As in the New Testament more generally, so in Paul's writings, the saving effect of Jesus' death is represented primarily through five constellations of images, each of which was borrowed from the public life of the ancient Mediterranean world:

- **the court of law**—for example, justification
- **the world of commerce**—for example, redemption
- **personal relationships**—for example, reconciliation
- **worship**—for example, sacrifice
- **the battleground**—for example, triumph over evil

Within these categories are clusters of terms, leading us to the conclusion that the significance of Jesus' death could not be represented by any one concept or theory or metaphor. Paul himself could write of substitution, representation, sacrifice, justification, forgiveness, reconciliation, triumph over the powers, redemption, and more. In the Letter to the Hebrews, on the other hand, the notion of sacrifice is paramount, with Jesus presented both as the perfect high priest who offers the sacrifice and as the perfect sacrificial victim. First Peter speaks of Jesus' death as a ransom and sacrifice, while the Book of Revelation presents Jesus' death in terms of military triumph and of redemption. And this list is only the beginning.

Rather than review this plethora of images, it may be more helpful to look more closely at Paul's theology of the cross. This will not only provide us with insight into the

2.

Make a list of the various images and models of the Atonement mentioned in this chapter. Add others that come to mind from your reading of Scripture. Which of these seems especially relevant to your community? Why?

witness of a central New Testament writer but will also orient us to a more focused discussion of what is at stake in this discussion of the work of Christ.

Paul and the Graciousness of God

It would be a grave error to imagine that the meaning of the cross focused on appeasing God's anger or winning God's merciful attention. One by one, the stories of human rebellion in Genesis 3–11—Adam and Eve, Cain and Abel, Noah and the ark, Babel—indicate that the human tendency toward sin is not matched by God's withdrawal. Rather, God draws near to see what humankind has done; pronounces judgment; then, in gracious optimism and mercy, tries again. The Scriptures as a whole provide no ground for a portrait of an angry God needing to be appeased in atoning sacrifice.

What, then, of the "wrath of God"? For Paul, "wrath" is not a quality of God's character. As he develops this concept in Romans 1, "wrath" is, rather, the active presence of God's judgment toward "all ungodliness and wickedness" (Romans 1:18). To speak of the wrath of God is not to speak of God's need "to get even" or to strike out in anger. Rather, it is the divine response to human unfaithfulness. God's wrath may be future, related to the end time (Romans 2:5, 7-8; Colossians 3:6; 1 Thessalonians 1:10; 5:9); but it is also already present, for God is now handing people over to experience the consequences of the sin they choose (Romans 1:18, 24, 26, 28). For Paul, then, God is not an angry deity requiring mollification. Divine wrath is not an affective quality or "feeling" on the part of God. Rather, it is a means of underscoring how seriously God takes sin. The righteousness of God is effective in the present to save; but as people resist it, they experience God's righteousness as condemnation.

Whatever else can be made of Paul's understanding of the death of Jesus, then, his theology of the cross lacks any elaboration on divine retribution. Quite the contrary, according to such texts as Romans 5:6-8, the death of Christ is the ultimate expression of the boundless love of

God: "God proves his love for us in that while we still were sinners Christ died for us."

In fact, Paul's affirmation in Romans 5 highlights three points that help us to gain even better perspective. First, the love of God for humanity is immeasurable; for there are no human parallels by which to understand it. Second, Paul's audience can be certain that their suffering has significance because the suffering of Christ has proven to be so meaningful. Through his death "we have been *justified*," "*saved* . . . from the wrath of God," "*reconciled* to God" (Romans 5:9-11). In the midst of our impotence, Christ took on the measure of our powerlessness and died in our place. As a result of his death, we share in his life; and we find that our own suffering has significance. Third, we are told that God demonstrates his love by means of what Christ did. We might have anticipated that God's love would be manifest best in God's own deed. This would certainly be the case if Paul were sketching an Atonement theology oriented toward divine recrimination, since in this case the cross would be nothing more or less than a divine lashing out against Jesus (rather than against all of humanity). Paul's way of putting things, however, shows the oneness of purpose and activity of God and God's Son in the cross.

At the same time, Paul's emphasis on God's initiative in salvation does not obviate his understanding of the need for atonement from the human side of the equation. Rather, his orientation toward God serves to introduce the sharp contrast Paul sees between God and humanity, that is, between the faithfulness of God and human unfaithfulness (see Romans 1:17-18). Paul's portrait of humanity "before Christ" is that of persons, collectively and individually, ensnared in sin, enslaved to powers from which they are impotent to escape.

Atonement and Reconciliation

Of the several dozen metaphors Paul uses to develop the meaning of the cross, several appear in 2 Corinthians 5:14–6:2. Here, then, is a helpful illustration of Paul's understanding of the cross.

A careful reading of 2 Corinthians 5:14–6:2 indicates

how Paul's interpretive categories overlap with one another. Even though reconciliation stands at the center of this passage, other images are also mentioned: vicarious substitution, representation, sacrifice, justification, forgiveness, and new creation. In addition, the cross and resurrection of Christ appear together as saving events.

Reconciliation as a term is not found very often in the Pauline corpus. Apart from this passage it appears in Romans 5:10-11 with reference to the reconciliation of humanity to God, in Colossians 1:20 with reference to the reconciliation of the cosmos to God, and in Ephesians 2:15-16 with reference to the reconciliation of both Jew and Gentile to God and one another. Some scholars do not think that Paul actually wrote Ephesians, but its message here is clearly Pauline. For in the writings of Paul, this notion of "restored relationship" consistently embraces the dynamic presence of love active to restore the divine-human relationship and to call persons to love one another in the same way. Moreover, especially in Second Corinthians and in Colossians, the work of reconciliation is extended to the entire creation.

Importantly, Paul does not speak here of any need for mutual reconciliation. "The world" is estranged from God and needs to be brought back into relationship with God. God, however, is not estranged from "the world." For this reason, Paul has no need to show how God can be appeased, how God might be empowered to love again, how God might overcome having been so often scorned, and so on. "In Christ God was reconciling the world to himself" (2 Corinthians 5:19)—this affirmation demonstrates that God's love has the upper hand in divine-human relations and that the work of Christ had as its effect the bringing of "the world" back to God (and not vice versa).

The Message of Salvation

In the face of this diversity of images, all of which help to spell out the meaning of Jesus' death, can something more be said about what is central to the work of Christ? In fact, some themes are pivotal; and New Testament presentations of the Atonement provide us with a set of questions to ask as we seek to understand and communicate the meaning of Jesus' death in new contexts. Although they leave plenty of room for creative theological reflection, they also provide critical points of orientation.

The first of these turns the spotlight on the human predicament. "Lostness" may be articulated in a variety of ways—blindness, deafness, hard-heartedness, slavery to an evil power, enmity, and so on—but one of the constants in the equation of New Testament thinking about the Atonement is the acute need of the human community. Humanity does not have the wherewithal to save itself but needs help (salvation, redemption, deliverance, and so on) from the outside, from God.

A second coordinate is the necessity of human response that flows out of the gracious act of God. The saving work of God has not yet run its full course, but the lives of God's people must already begin to reflect the new reality (or new creation) to which God is moving history. We are saved *from*, it is true; but we are also saved *for*. Atonement theology in the New Testament does not simply hold tightly to the work of Christ but opens wide its arms to embrace and guide the lives of Christians. Believers—having been redeemed, reconciled, delivered, bought, justified, and so on—are now released and empowered to reflect in their lives the quality of life exemplified by their Savior. This life is modeled after the cross and has service as its basic orientation. Atonement *theology* cannot be separated from *ethics*.

Between the human predicament and the imperative of human response is the divine drama, the ultimate manifestation of the love of God. This is the third coordinate: God, acting on the basis of his covenant love, on his own initiative, was at work in the cross of Christ for human salvation. The New Testament portrays Golgotha along two storylines—one with God as subject, the other with Jesus as subject. It will not do, therefore, to characterize the Atonement as God's punishment falling on Christ (that is, God as subject, Christ as object) or as Christ's appeasement or persuasion of God (Christ as subject, God as object). At the same time, however paradoxical it may seem, what happened on

3,

Imagine that your assignment this week is to prepare and present a lesson on the saving significance of the cross for the high school youth group. How would you sketch "The Message of Salvation" in a way that took seriously the life experiences and language patterns of your audience?

the cross for our atonement was, according to the New Testament, a consequence of God's initiative, a demonstration of divine love. As Paul summarizes, employing one model among many possibilities, "In Christ God was reconciling the world to himself" (2 Corinthians 5:19). Again, "God proves his love for us in that while we still were sinners Christ died for us" (Romans 5:8).

Fourth, and as a corollary to the three previous themes, New Testament Atonement theology accords privilege to no one group over another. What happened on the cross was of universal significance—in the language of the day, for Jew and Gentile, for slave and free, for male and female. The cross was the expression of God's grace for all, for all persons as well as for all creation. Atonement theology thus repudiates ancient and modern attempts at segregating people away from the gracious invitation of God or otherwise possessing as one's own the gift of God available to all humanity.

8

The Way of the Cross

Key Concepts:
- In what ways did Paul experience suffering in the context of his apostolic mission?
- How did Paul understand the relationship between his own suffering and the suffering of Christ?
- How does the cross help to define the nature of authentic Christian community?
- What perspective on the cross and human suffering does the Book of Revelation provide?
- How would you define the "way of the cross"?

What are we to make of a community of faith that takes its central identity from an instrument of gruesome execution, a people for whom the cross serves as rallying point? One answer has focused on the immeasurable good that comes from the cross of Christ. The message that "Christ died for our sins" has sometimes been enough to allow Jesus' followers to look beyond the abhorrent realities of crucifixion. At the same time, even during his own lifetime, Jesus spoke as though his fate on the cross was somehow intermingled with the lives and destiny of his followers. "If any want to become my followers, let them deny themselves and take up their cross and follow me" (Mark 8:34).

The work of Christ on the cross has always been understood by Christians as for our salvation. The New

Testament is also brimming with evidence that the cross of Christ was embraced as the norm of discipleship. What this means is the concern of this chapter.

The Cross of Christ and the Suffering of Paul

One way to grasp further the significance of Jesus' passion and death is to follow Paul's own career, which was stamped with suffering on account of his unrelenting commitment to Christ. In Second Corinthians, Paul summarizes his experience as an apostle: "We are afflicted in every way, but not crushed; perplexed, but not driven to despair; persecuted, but not forsaken; struck down, but not destroyed; always carrying in the body the death of Jesus" (4:8-10).

The apostle also speaks in general but poignant terms of his persecution when he asks, "Why am I still being persecuted?" (Galatians 5:11) and then dramatically asserts, most probably with reference to the marks of his persecution, "I carry the marks of Jesus branded on my body" (6:17).

The Persecuted Apostle

Elsewhere Paul was more specific in his images and reports. In 1 Corinthians 4:9, he observes that apostles are like people condemned to death in the arena. This was a Roman form of penalty, in which people were condemned to death through combat with gladiators or wild beasts in great Roman amphitheaters. According to the Jewish historian Josephus, Herod Agrippa had forced some 1400 people of his realm to fight to their deaths in his amphitheater at Berytus.[1] Paul apparently used this imagery to denote the life-and-death struggle of apostles engaged in the pursuit of their commission.

According to Acts 14:8-20, Paul was stoned at Lystra. Stoning was a form of capital punishment among Jewish people in cases of cursing or slandering the name of Yahweh (Leviticus 24:15-16), performing sorcery or wizardry (Exodus 22:18; Leviticus 20:27), violating the sabbath

(Exodus 31:14-15; Numbers 15:32-36), and encouraging allegiance to or worship of idols (Deuteronomy 13:6-10). Although someone like Paul, who challenged the status quo of Israelite religion, might well have been regarded as deserving capital punishment, stoning could also be an expression of popular anger and mob violence.

Paul also notes that he was imprisoned repeatedly, and his testimony coheres with that of Acts (for example, 2 Corinthians 6:5; 11:23; Colossians 4:10; Philemon; see Acts 16:23-40). He also suffered corporal punishment from Jewish and Roman leaders, including being whipped with rods and scourging (Acts 16:22; 22:24-25; 2 Corinthians 6:5; 11:24). In 2 Corinthians 11:23-27, Paul outlines his suffering in terms of labors, imprisonments, countless floggings, scourging, beating with rods, stoning, shipwreck, constant danger on the road, toil, hardship, sleeplessness, hunger, and thirst.

For many of us, merely the beginnings of persecution of this magnitude would result in immediate stock taking. "What have I done to deserve this?" we might ask. Paul's problems in this regard were compounded further, however; for he faced Christians at Corinth who regarded his abundant suffering as positive proof that he could not be a genuine apostle. How could the hand of God and the power of the Spirit be on someone who attracted this level of hostility? Would God lead someone into this kind of harm? Would God not protect those whom he had commissioned?

Paul and the Way of the Cross

Paul's first response was to provide at several points in his Corinthian correspondence a "catalog of circumstances," a list of his experiences in the mission (see 1 Corinthians 4:9-13; 2 Corinthians 4:7-12; 6:3-10; 11:23-33; 12:10). Moralists and philosophers of his day might do the same in order to indicate their personal merit, to show how well they performed under pressure. Stoics, for example, might list hardships in order to dismiss them as inconsequential. Public figures might present their impressive achievements as ennobling credentials. Others might list their adversities

1.

For Paul, how does "the way of the cross" compare with "the way of this world"? If this comparison were to be made today, how would it differ?

in order to demonstrate how they had overcome affliction, in a kind of rags-to-riches story. In listing his hardships, however, Paul made no attempt to lessen their drain on his life and work or otherwise to dismiss them as inconsequential. Nor did Paul in any way suggest how he had overcome adversity or even that he had done so. Quite the contrary; Paul seemed to wear his suffering and hardship as a badge of honor. It was precisely in his being persecuted that he demonstrated that he was a genuine follower of Christ. His emphasis was not on power overcoming or transcending weakness but on the power of God expressed in weakness.

Paul's message at this point seemed counterintuitive among the Corinthians, and it may seem so to us. Within the Roman world, honor was a precious commodity; and people gave themselves to its pursuit. Following the prescribed conventions of society and cultivating socially determined virtues— these were (and are) the routes to honor. Paul found in the cross of Christ a competing definition of honor. Honor before God comes through identification with Christ, and identification with Christ cannot bypass the cross.

Did this make Paul a masochist? Was Paul looking for trouble so that he would achieve glory before God? Hardly. The way of the cross as this was sketched in Paul's life was not the way of sorrows; it was not an invitation to pain and suffering. In fact, it is important to realize that Paul was not about the business of embracing persecution. Nor should it be imagined that Jesus went looking for the cross and happily embraced its arduous suffering. Rather, Jesus devoted himself unreservedly to serving the purpose of God. Because he did so "in this adulterous and sinful generation" (Mark 8:38), he found himself increasingly at odds with the ruling elite of his day, both Jewish and Roman. His eyes were focused on God's will; but the road to God's will for Jesus led through Golgotha, the Place of the Skull where he was crucified. Though the details were different, the same could be said for Paul. His bottom line was not persecution but fidelity to his commission and to the gospel. These led him into conflict, especially with the Jewish people, sometimes even with Christians who were unwilling to embrace the radical nature of the gospel, and finally with Rome.

Clearly, then, Paul regarded suffering as the authentication of his apostolic ministry and the way of the cross as the heart of discipleship. How can this be? We can synthesize his perspective with the following affirmations:

- Followers of Christ should expect opposition. God's messengers in the Old and New Testaments regularly encountered opposition as a result of their witness to the ways of God in a world pursuing its own ways.
- Followers of Christ must follow the way of Christ. In his suffering, Paul expressed his essential unity with Christ in his core commitments and, thus, in the working out of the power of the crucified Messiah in Paul's ministry.
- Those who follow the way of the cross participate in the sufferings of Christ. Building on the Jewish notion of the woes that would accompany the birthing of the messianic age, the suffering of those who follow the Messiah brings forward the triumph of divine love and salvation. As Paul remarks in Colossians 1:24, "In my flesh I am completing what is lacking in Christ's afflictions for the sake of his body, that is, the church."

The Cross and the Christian Community

Paul's perspective on the way of the cross was not limited to his own experience. The death of Christ marked the beginning of a new era, and this fundamentally changes the way one understands life in the present. First, awareness that Christ's death and resurrection have instituted a new epoch allows one to envision new life in contrast to old ways of living and to embrace the power of God requisite for new life. Moreover, considering the present in light of the past motivates believers to act in gratitude for deliverance from slavery to sin. Finally and most importantly for our reflection here, recognition of this new time encourages believers' further recognition that life in the present is determined by the cross. This means that one effect of the cross is the possibility of restored humanity—restored in its relationships to God, to itself, and to all creation. It also means that the definition of existence put forward by sinful humanity has been radically altered, so that those who follow Christ must look to Christ for the expression of restored humanity. The church whose theology is shaped by the message of the cross must live out its faith in ways that reflect the cross; otherwise, its theology carries no credibility.

What this means practically is related above all to believers taking on themselves the form of obedience to God represented in Christ's life, expressed ultimately in his death. This thought lies behind Paul's use of the hymn to Christ in Philippians 2:6-11. It also lies behind his defense of his own apostolic ministry, his sense that in his weakness and suffering he was engaged in the imitation of Christ and participation in the suffering of the Messiah. Paul did not regard himself as unique in this regard. Philippians 2 urges practices of humility and selflessness (2:1-5) with reference to the examples of Christ Jesus (2:6-11), Paul (2:17-18), Timothy (2:19 24), and Epaphroditus (2:25-30).

Paul's emphasis on lives of humility and power in weakness was rooted in the cross. As such it crossed the grain of the dominant ethos-informing practices in the Roman world. The cross was an instrument of shame. How could it serve positively and as a paradigm for any Roman? Paul subverted the world order through his theology of the cross. God gives freely and abundantly; moreover, he gives even to those who oppose his ways. The cross is thus positioned as the means of reconciliation but also as the exemplar of a way of life lived for others. In this way Paul commends a politics, an ordering of power, a way of living distinct from and indeed opposed to the politics of his world and ours.

The cross of Christ has as its effect the transformation of humanity in another sense, too. Paul understood the cross as a boundary-shattering event. Thus, Paul could assert in First Corinthians that those who follow the example of Christ in his selfless death will not nurture their status-based divisions within the Christian community but will gain a fuller understanding and appreciation of the body of Christ (1 Corinthians 11:17–12:31). This, after all, is a manifestation of the new covenant in Christ's blood (1 Corinthians 11:25). But Paul could also assert that faithful identification with Christ in his saving work opposes even more fundamental ethnic, social, and sexual boundaries; "for in Christ Jesus you are all children of God through faith" (Galatians 3:26-29; compare Ephesians 2:11-22). In this way too, then, the cross not only enables new life but also points beyond itself to disclose new norms of that life.

The Way of the Cross and the Lamb of God

The definition of Christian life as "cruciform," modeled on the unswerving faithfulness of Jesus Christ and imitating the humility and selflessness he displayed on the cross, pervades the New Testament. Peter went so far as to ground his directive to "live as free people" (1 Peter 2:16; that is, to show honor to everyone) in the suffering of Christ: "For to this you have been called, because Christ also suffered for you, leaving you an example, so that you should follow in his steps" (1 Peter 2:21). By way of illustrating this concern further, the perspective of the Book of Revelation is especially important.

Chapters 2–3 of Revelation contain seven letters to seven churches, all located in the region we now know as eastern Turkey. These letters address a series of concerns particular to each church and demonstrate that the Book of Revelation, when it was first written, was focused on more than one kind of audience. Some indeed were suffering for their faith; but others, who had assimilated themselves more fully into the Roman Empire, were prospering in the world. In the Book of Revelation, John provides a word of encouragement for the one group, a word of criticism and challenge for the other.

On the horizon, John saw a time of great calamity that would test the faithfulness of his readers. He paints the end-time mural with stark images of warfare and calls his audience "to overcome." How are followers of Christ to engage in warfare? How are they to triumph? One of the

2.

Faithful witness in the world requires prophetic engagement with the world, irrespective of the consequences. What sort of local church mission statement might grow out of such a claim?

options available in recent memory would have been the way of the Zealots, whose revolutionary activity played so significant a role in the conflict between Jews and Rome in the A.D. 60's. In the case of the Zealots, resistance against Rome took the shape of violent, militaristic activity. Another option was that of the sectarians at Qumran. They also opposed the cultural reforms and rule of outsiders like Rome. Their resistance took the form of removal from society at large into the desert where they could maintain a community of holiness. John advised neither of these options but nevertheless called for resistance. What form did his "third way" take?

Simply put, John placed before his readers the way of the Lamb. What does this mean? In the Book of Revelation, the Lamb is the chief Christological image; and its meaning comes into sharpest focus in Revelation 5. Here John narrates a scene of high drama, initially tragic in its attempt to locate the one authorized to break the seal and to open the scroll held in God's right hand. How will the sovereignty of God be established if no one can open the scroll and reveal its contents? There is only one who is qualified; and he is identified first as "the Lion of the tribe of Judah, the Root of David" (5:5), that is, the triumphant and militaristic Messiah of God. When John focuses his eyes on this Lion, however, what he sees is a slaughtered Lamb, whose worthiness to open the scroll, we quickly discover, is grounded in the manner and significance of his death:

> You are worthy to take the scroll
>   and to open its seals,
> for you were slaughtered and by
>   your blood you ransomed for God
> saints from every tribe and
>   language and people and nation.
>   (Revelation 5:9)

What is fascinating about this paradox of images is that they coexist without contradiction in one person. Jesus is the conquering Messiah, and the manner of his victory is his slaughter. Jesus' death is evil's defeat.

Central to John's interpretation of the death of Jesus is its effectiveness in defeating evil. Revelation places the drama of salvation on the cosmic stage, so that the slaughter of the Lamb wins a cosmic victory. The technology of this warfare goes unidentified; specifically how the cross overcomes evil is not developed. What is clear is that the faithfulness of Jesus in his life-giving death is a faithfulness to the eternal will of God. The death of Jesus shows how God measures fidelity and triumph; and, because God is the uncontested sovereign of the universe, Jesus' faithfulness in the cross repeals all other powers, all other purposes.

Those who worship the Lamb are called to embrace the way of the Lamb, to emulate in their lives the faithful witness of the Lamb—even to the death. This note is sounded especially in Revelation 12:11:

> They have conquered [Satan] by
>   the blood of the Lamb
>   and by the word of their testimony,
> for they did not cling to life even
>   in the face of death.

John presents here no call to masochistic martyrdom; he does not idealize suffering and death. Instead, he insists that faithful witness in the world requires prophetic engagement with the world, irrespective of the consequences. We may recall that John himself had been exiled to Patmos "because of the word of God and the testimony of Jesus" (Revelation 1:9). Although he had not been martyred, John's own faithful witness had invited the malevolent attention of the same forces that had placed Jesus on the cross.

Taking up the Cross

What we have seen in the letters of Paul and in the Revelation of John is only the outworking of the perspective on his own death that Jesus had articulated for his disciples. "Christology" is intricately related to "discipleship." As one views the Messiah, so one views the nature of discipleship. To name Jesus as Messiah is to embark on a life's journey that is messianic, in the sense that it emulates the life, the commitments, and the dispositions of the Messiah.

Within the narrative of the first three Gospels, this is spelled out in unmistakable terms. In Mark's Gospel, for example, Peter denounces Jesus for defining his messianic mission in terms of suffering death, only to learn from Jesus that, as dreadful as his destiny would be, those who would choose to follow him could expect nothing other than the opposition that would become Jesus' trademark by the end of his life (Mark 8:27-38). In this context, "denying oneself" is especially related to how one understands and constructs one's identity. One's family heritage, the status that comes with one's work, one's resumé of qualifications—all these and more are trivialized in favor of identification with Christ and participation in the community of those who follow him. "Taking up the cross," when understood literally, depicts discipleship as the life of those whose lives are forfeit, who are already on the way to their place of execution. Personal rights, feelings of envy, grasping for recognition—these and all other personal agenda have no place for the person who is only minutes away from death. In Luke's Gospel, "taking up the cross" cannot be understood in such literal terms; for here Jesus directs his would-be followers to take up the cross *daily* (Luke 9:23). This suggests a form of life governed by the metaphor of living under a death sentence—not in the sense of living with gloom or listlessness, but with appropriate perspective with regard to what really matters in life.

Jesus' message thus portends for his followers a life like his own. His focus on cross bearing is not concerned with suffering for the sake of suffering but highlights how God's salvation will permeate the whole world. Those who, like Jesus, are ready to deny themselves and take up the cross are no longer burdened by the requirements and cravings that characterize the world. Here is a theology of the cross that is not so much concerned with a theory of the Atonement as with a narrative portrayal of the messianic life as the way of the cross.

3.

What are some of the marks of persons who have denied themselves, taken up the cross daily, and followed Jesus? Would we esteem such persons? Do we? Please explain.

[1] From *Jewish Antiquities*, by Josephus; 19.7.5.

9

Raised to Life

Key Concepts:

- In what ways does the Old Testament prepare for the New Testament proclamation of the resurrection of Jesus from the dead?
- What evidence do we have for the empty tomb?
- Is there additional historical testimony for the resurrection of Jesus?
- How do the Gospels understand the significance of the message of Jesus' resurrection?
- How does Paul work out the importance of Jesus' resurrection for the faith and life of the church?
- What role does the resurrection of Jesus by God play in our understanding of the nature of Jesus' person and message?

With the demise of their leader, it is easy to imagine that the circle of Jesus' disciples would simply have disbanded, with its members returning to their former lives. The Jewish historian Josephus records the rise of other prophetic and messianic figures in the first-century period. Perhaps, like those others, the movement centered on Jesus was counterfeit.

Demoralized and with hopes dashed, the disciples appear apprehensive and without purpose in the hours immediately following the Crucifixion. The portrait of the disciples in the early chapters of Acts demonstrates, however, that what could have happened, what perhaps should have happened, did not happen. Faith in Jesus not only continued, it grew. In the pages of Acts, Jesus' witnesses speak boldly of their leader, even placing their own lives at risk to do so. How can we explain this outcome?

After the death of Jesus, two events proved to be pivotal for the ongoing life and ministry of the church. The first of these was the resurrection of Jesus, and the second was the outpouring of the Holy Spirit. The first was the powerful act of God, validating Jesus' identity as God's Son and demonstrating the true nature of Jesus' work. The second was the act of Jesus, demonstrating at Pentecost and subsequently that, far from ending with his death on the cross, Jesus' work would and must continue, and with power. Both acts placed the cross of Christ in proper perspective.

This does not mean that the focus of the early church on its resurrection theology moved Jesus' crucifixion into the shadows of historical misfortune. The New Testament does not portray the cross as a tragedy that had to be overturned by resurrection power. The cross was no hiccup in God's plan, a catastrophic afterthought that had to be overcome. Hence, the significance of the Resurrection does not lie in its capacity to annul the misfortune of Jesus' crucifixion. The Resurrection did not occur in spite of the cross but was the ultimate confirmation that the ministry and message of Jesus, including his death on the cross, were in fact manifestations of God's own purpose. God's will is seen in Jesus' works of healing and exorcism, in his teaching and table practices, in his calling of disciples, and even in his death. How do we know? The Resurrection is God's validation of Jesus' life, his person, and his ministry.

The outpouring of the Spirit is closely related, for the coming of the Spirit (1) proves that Jesus has indeed been raised from the dead and (2) provides the leadership and direction for the church's continuation of Jesus' ministry. But the relationship of Christ and the Spirit, and the implications of that relationship for discipleship and mission, are the subject of Chapter 10. Here we are concerned with the resurrection of Jesus.

Interpreting "Resurrection"

According to the Book of Acts, news of Jesus' resurrection was central to the proclamation of the early church. For example, in the first public address recounted in Acts, Peter affirmed Jesus' status as Lord and Christ with reference to his resurrection. Of course, from this perspective Jesus became nothing at the Resurrection that he was not already; at his birth the angels declared that he was Savior, Messiah, and Lord (Luke 2:11). During his ministry, however, the exalted status of Jesus signified by these titles was not understood even by his followers. Moreover, it was rejected by the Jerusalem elite who were instrumental in bringing about what must have been regarded as decisive proof against Jesus' exalted status, namely, his execution on a Roman cross. Jesus' resurrection thus serves to validate the status Jesus possessed already but that was in doubt on account of his maltreatment in Jerusalem. In Peter's Pentecost sermon, the proof of Jesus' resurrection comes in three parts: (1) David the prophet spoke of Jesus' resurrection and enthronement as Messiah (Acts 2:25-31); (2) Peter and the other apostles are themselves witnesses of Jesus' resurrection (Acts 2:32); and (3) the phenomena associated with the outpouring of the Spirit ("that you both see and hear") are the consequence of Jesus' exaltation and reception of the promise of the Spirit (Acts 2:33). The Christology of Peter's sermon is marked by God's irrefutable vindication of Jesus' identity, even to the point that Jesus is now regarded as coregent with God in the gracious provision of the blessings of salvation.

Elsewhere, too, Jesus' disciples make Jesus' resurrection the central affirmation in their proclamation. Paul wrote, "If Christ has not been raised, then our proclamation has been in vain and your faith has been in vain" (1 Corinthians 15:14), just as Peter wrote, "By his great mercy he has given us a new birth into a living hope through the resurrection of Jesus Christ from the dead" (1 Peter 1:3). This raises an important question. Given that the resurrection of Jesus was pivotal for Christian faith, how would people in the first-century Mediterranean world have made sense of the news of Jesus' resurrection? What categories of interpretation would have helped them to understand the message of resurrection? Sharply put, what is "resurrection"?

The idea of resurrection from the dead belongs to the

later frontiers of Israel's faith, according to the Old Testament. Numerous texts record the burial of the dead (for example, Genesis 50:13; Joshua 24:32) without mentioning the fate of the dead. In Israel's Scriptures, *Sheol* does appear as the place of the dead, where the dead have a shadowy existence in a common abode.

Hints of resurrection faith occur in a handful of prophetic texts. For example, in Hosea 6:1-3 we read of the prospect of the revival of God's people:

> Come, let us return to the LORD;
>   for it is he who has torn, and
>   he will heal us;
>   he has struck down, and he
>   will bind us up.
> After two days he will revive us;
>   on the third day he will raise us up,
>   that we might live before him.
> Let us know, let us press on to
>   know the LORD;
>   his appearing is as sure as the dawn;
> he will come to us like the showers,
>   like the spring rains that water the earth.

This prophecy attracted the attention of the church fathers, who read in it a prophecy of Jesus' resurrection on the third day; and early Jewish interpretation found here a reference to the end-time resurrection of Israel. In its own eighth-century context, its meaning may not have been so clear, however. "Raising up" is more likely to refer metaphorically to the restoration of the nation than to the literal raising up of persons whose life on this earth had ended.

Ezekiel 37:1-14, with its dramatic image of the valley of dry bones brought to life, also provides a vision of Israel's restoration. This did not keep later Jewish interpretation from finding here a graphic depiction of the resurrection, however. Note especially verses 12-13: "I am going to . . . bring you up from your graves." In both of these texts—one from Hosea, the other from Ezekiel—we find the interweaving of the promise of Israel's restoration with the recreative work of the Lord.

Many scholars find a more direct reference to resurrection in Isaiah 26:19:

> Your dead shall live,
>> their corpses shall rise.
> O dwellers in the dust,
>> awake and sing for joy!
> For your dew is a radiant dew,
>> and the earth will give birth to
>>> those long dead.

Like the vision in Ezekiel 37, Isaiah's words appear in a context that proposes Israel's restoration and, indeed, exaltation among the nations. With regard to the meaning of this text in particular, the debate centers on whether a literal raising up of dead corpses is envisioned. At the very least, however, we have here in Isaiah a further text that relates the notion of resurrection to the activity of God by which he restores and exalts his people and by which he pours upon them the totality of his covenant blessings.

The first unambiguous reference to the physical resurrection of the dead appears in Daniel 12:1-3:

> At that time Michael, the great prince, the protector of your people, shall arise. There shall be a time of anguish, such as has never occurred since nations first came into existence. But at that time your people shall be delivered, everyone who is found written in the book. Many of those who sleep in the dust of the earth shall awake, some to everlasting life, and some to shame and everlasting contempt. Those who are wise shall shine like the brightness of the sky, and those who lead many to righteousness, like the stars forever and ever.

This passage forms the climax of the revelation that began in Daniel 11:2 and marks the decisive triumph of God's people over the enemies of Israel. At last, Israel will experi-

1.

*The signifi-
cance of the
resurrection
of Jesus for
his first fol-
lowers grew
out of its sig-
nal impor-
tance within
the grand
mural of
God's deal-
ings with and
promises to
Israel. To
what degree
do we iden-
tify with
ancient Israel
and its hopes?
How does this
affect our
understand-
ing of the
importance of
the resurrec-
tion of Jesus?*

ence salvation in its fullest sense. Not all will experience this deliverance, however, but only those found in "the book" (that is, the book of life; compare Isaiah 4:3; Malachi 3:16-18). Others will experience the resurrection as judgment. It is in this way that Daniel's concern with the vindication of God's righteous servants comes into clearest focus.

When we take these texts into account, together with additional Jewish material written in the era of the Second Temple, several motifs begin to surface; and these help us to know what categories of interpretation might have been available to those who first heard of Jesus' resurrection:

- Resurrection signals the restoration of Israel.
- Resurrection signals Israel's triumph over its enemies. (Taken together, these first two motifs speak of the experience of conclusive and end-time salvation among the people of God.)
- Resurrection marks God's vindication of the righteous who have suffered unjustly. Having been condemned and made to suffer by a human court, the righteous will in the resurrection be vindicated in the divine court.
- Resurrection marks the decisive establishment of divine justice, where rewards and punishments are meted out in relation to the character of one's life before death. Injustice and wickedness will not have the final word but in the resurrection will be decisively repudiated.

Evidence for the Resurrection of Jesus

According to the New Testament, no one actually witnessed the Resurrection event itself; yet the unanimous witness of the New Testament materials is that Jesus is alive, beyond the grave. The lack of eyewitnesses to this event does not mean that we lack any evidence for Jesus' resurrection but only that the evidence available to us is indirect. Especially important in this regard is the empty tomb of Jesus.

Each of the Gospels records the death and burial of Jesus, and each includes a scene in which the tomb in which he was buried is found to be empty. What is startling is that, again according to the unanimous testimony of the

Gospels, the first witnesses of the empty tomb were women. This is startling because of the generally low esteem in which the testimony of women was typically held at that time. Women in the ancient world were generally not highly regarded and were not sought out to provide legal testimony. Hence, it seems highly improbable that early Christians would have featured women in an invented story. Luke's report is nearer the mark when it observes that the apostles first regarded the women's report of the empty tomb as sheer nonsense (Luke 24:11).

It is also interesting that nothing in the New Testament indicates that anyone doubted that the tomb was empty. Consider, for example, Matthew's account. First, extra guards were placed in position in order to ensure that the body of Jesus could not be abducted. Then, when the tomb was found to be empty, a plan was concocted and guards were bribed in order to spread the story that Jesus' body had been stolen by his disciples (Matthew 27:62-66; 28:11-15). Although the agenda of this conspiracy was to call into question announcements of Jesus' resurrection, it actually confirmed the empty tomb. In this instance, no one denied that the tomb was empty but instead tried to explain away this fact.

In addition, it is remarkable that there is no evidence at all that Jesus' followers set up a shrine for worship at his place of burial in the decades following his death. After all, praying at the tomb of other heroes of the faith was a well-established practice. Why was there no veneration of Jesus' tomb, unless it was widely recognized that his tomb was empty?

It is little wonder, then, that in his book *Jesus the Jew* (1973), the noted Jewish historian and Oxford University professor Geza Vermes concludes his own examination of the evidence with the assertion that when the women set out to pay their last respects to Jesus, they found to their alarm not a body, but an empty tomb.[1]

Historical evidence in support of the message of the Resurrection comes from two additional sources. The first includes the repeated assurances in the New Testament that people experienced encounters with the risen Lord and that this experience utterly changed their lives. Indeed, something must explain the transformation of the disciples that occurred so quickly following the Crucifixion from an aimless, deflated, fractured company to the cohesive, hopeful, and purpose-driven band of followers.

Second, the evidence we surveyed above provides no indication of any expectation of the resurrection of a single person. Moreover, since we search in vain for a prophecy of a Messiah who would die, we also lack any evidence for a Messiah who would be raised from the dead. Among those Jews who did look forward to the resurrection (a view that was not universally held; see Acts 23:8), "resurrection" entailed the *general* resurrection, that is, the resurrection of which Daniel speaks: "Many of those who sleep in the dust of the earth shall awake, some to everlasting life, and some to shame and everlasting contempt" (12:2). In short, the very idea that one person would be raised from the dead goes against what we know about the resurrection beliefs of the Jewish people. That such an odd idea would have been constructed and broadcast and that it would have gained acceptance is difficult to imagine.

According to Acts, Jesus, after his death, "presented himself alive to [his disciples] by many convincing proofs" (1:3). For the earliest disciples, it was clearly important that the good news be grounded in the historical reality of the resurrection of Jesus from the dead. That Jesus was raised from the dead is only part of the story, however. It was also important to grapple with the meaning of Jesus' resurrection within the redemptive plan of God.

Interpreting the Resurrection of Jesus

All four Gospels describe the discovery of the empty tomb; and the Gospels of Matthew, Luke, and John go on to narrate stories in which Jesus appears to his disciples. In doing so, the writers of the Gospels are concerned with more than reporting "just the facts." They wrap the resurrection of Jesus in interpretive clothing. First, they tie the resurrection of Jesus into the story of Jesus' life and especially into Jesus' own predictions of his resurrection.

Second, they weave the resurrection of Jesus into Israel's faith, Israel's Scriptures, and the purpose of God. In telling the story, each Gospel promotes its own emphases.

All four Gospels emphasize first the faithfulness of women. Jesus' (male) disciples are conspicuous by their absence in relation to the burial and to the discovery of the empty tomb. In order to illustrate how the Gospels develop further the significance of Jesus' resurrection, we can turn our attention briefly to the endings of the Gospels of Matthew and Mark.

Matthew's Gospel contains apocalyptic overtones; that is, it presents the Resurrection as an end-time event in which divine deliverance is disclosed. Of course, the Jewish notion of resurrection itself points in this direction; but in Matthew this emphasis is heightened by the great earthquake at the rolling back of the stone and the description of the appearance of the angel of the Lord at the tomb (Matthew 28:2-3; compare Daniel 7:9; 10:6). Matthew's account also places a premium on verifying the empty tomb. The angel invites a closer look at the tomb (28:6), and the Evangelist describes the Jewish plan both to ensure that Jesus' body was not stolen (27:62-66) and to conceal the fact that it had not been stolen (28:11-15). These points present the empty tomb as an incontrovertible fact at the same time that they underscore the reliability of Jesus' prophecy of his own resurrection. The physicality of the Resurrection is noted in passing, as the Evangelist refers to the disciples' taking hold of Jesus' feet (28:9). The resurrected Lord is no phantom. Finally, Matthew emphasizes the reconstitution of the community of Jesus' followers, their worship of Jesus, and their commissioning by him.

Early Greek manuscripts differ in their representation of the ending of the Gospel of Mark, but the best evidence available from those manuscripts leads us to believe today that the Gospel ended with 16:8 (and thus did not include the other endings typically included as possibilities in modern English translations). As a result, Mark's Gospel recounts an empty tomb scene but includes no resurrection appearances. Two emphases come to the fore. First, continuity is established. Jesus had predicted that the disciples would be scattered, then regathered in Galilee after his resurrection (Mark 14:27-28). They were scattered at his arrest, and then the angel confirmed that Jesus had indeed been raised and would meet his disciples in Galilee. All this happened "just as he told you" (16:7). Second, and closely related, Mark's narrative implies that the failure of the women to report the message of the angel (16:8) was not really the end of the story. Although the failure of Jesus' disciples is a recurring motif in the Gospel of Mark, the ending of Mark leaves open the possibility that they will respond with discernment and faithfulness. Indeed, in light of the reliability of Jesus' prophecies to this point of the narrative, Jesus' promise to meet his followers in Galilee fully anticipates that the story of Jesus will lead into the story of the ongoing faithful mission of the disciples.

We have already mentioned the difficulty posed by the resurrection of an individual, Jesus, within the context of resurrection theologies in first-century Judaism. How does one square the resurrection of one person with the expectation of a general resurrection, that is, with the resurrection of the many? Paul contributes significantly to our understanding at this point by describing Jesus' resurrection as the guarantee of the general resurrection. In this way, Paul interprets the resurrection of Jesus as a genuinely end-time event, which sets in motion the end-time promises of God. Additionally, Paul does so in a way that shows the importance of Jesus' resurrection for our understanding of life on both sides of the grave.

2.

What is the significance of Jesus' resurrection for Christian belief today?

Paul's most sustained discussion of the resurrection appears in 1 Corinthians 15—in a letter where he is concerned with divisions within the Corinthian community (1 Corinthians 1:10) and in a chapter where he is struggling to spell out the nature of resurrection life. The divisions with which Paul was concerned were both social and philosophical and were related to different views of what happens after death. Following customary practice in the Roman world, persons of wealth and status in Corinth would have extended hospitality to itinerant philosophers and thus have been exposed to more sophisticated notions about the afterlife. For them, Paul's talk of the raising of the dead would have been reminiscent of fables about the resuscitation of corpses, the stuff of popular myths. Taught to degrade the body, these people would have found Paul's teaching about the resurrection incomprehensible, even ridiculous. Those of relative poverty and low status, on the other hand, would have been incapable of welcoming itinerant philosophers into their homes and thus would have lived apart from their influence. They would have had closer contact with superstitions and popular myths, including those relating the resuscitation of corpses and the endowment of those corpses with immortality. Since Paul's primary objective in First Corinthians was to restore unity (1:10), his challenge was to represent the resurrection belief of early Christianity with enough sophistication to communicate effectively with those of high status while not alienating those of lower status.

It is in 1 Corinthians 15:35-58 that Paul discusses the nature of the resurrection; and in doing so he affirms the following: (1) There is a profound continuity between present life in this world and life everlasting with God. For human beings, this continuity has to do with bodily existence. That is, Paul cannot think in terms of a free-floating soul separate from a body. (2) Present human existence, however, is marked by frailty, deterioration, weakness, and is therefore unsuited for eternal life. Therefore, in order for Christian believers to share in eternal life, their bodies must be transformed. Paul does not here think of "immortality of the soul." Neither does he proclaim a resuscitation of dead bodies that might serve as receptacles for souls that had escaped the body in death. Instead, he sets before his audience the promise of the transformation of their bodies into glorified bodies (compare Philippians 3:21). (3) Paul's ideas are, in part, rooted in images from the natural world and, in part, related to the resurrection of Jesus Christ. As it was with Christ's body, Paul insists, so it will be with ours: the same, yet not the same; transformed for the new conditions of life with God forever. (4) For Paul, this has important meaning for the nature of Christian life in the present. For example, this message underscores the significance of life in this world—a fact that many

Christians at Corinth had not taken seriously. We should not imagine that our bodies are unimportant, then, or that what we do to our bodies or with our bodies is somehow unrelated to eternal life (compare Colossians 1:24). The idea of eternal life is not escapism. Rather, it provides the Christian with hope as well as with a vision of what is important to God. As a result, we may look forward to the future while also allowing this vision of the future to help determine the nature of our lives in the present.

Resurrection, Salvation, and Commission

What is the importance of the Resurrection for Christian faith and life? Most fundamentally, the resurrection of Jesus is God's own ratification of Jesus' message and ministry, identifying him incontrovertibly as the unique Son of God and validating his message of a life lived for others.

This means that the cross (which is the decisive expression of the character of Jesus' life) and the Resurrection are mutually interpreting and confirming. We affirm that the cross of Christ is the resolute disclosure of God's redemptive grace, and we can affirm this because we are speaking of the cross of the one whom God raised from the dead. Similarly, we affirm that the resurrection of Jesus is God's powerful act to save precisely because we are speaking of the resurrection of the crucified one. Jesus of Nazareth, crucified, dead, and buried, is the exalted Lord.

3.

What is the significance of Jesus' resurrection for the church's mission today?

Additionally, the Resurrection marks in a definite way the changing of the times, the inauguration of the period of the restoration of the people of God. Today, we live in the shadow of the cross, to be sure, so that our lives are to be marked by the selflessness and orientation to the divine purpose that characterized the life of Jesus. But we also live in anticipation of the transformation of all things, guaranteed by God's raising of Jesus from the dead.

It sometimes too easily escapes our attention that the resurrection of Jesus is not only a cause for celebration but also contains within itself a missionary mandate. Appearing to his disciples after his resurrection, Jesus, according to Matthew's Gospel, tied together his training of his disciples with their commission to go and make disciples of all nations (Matthew 28:19-20). Jesus, according to the opening of Acts, spent some forty days with his followers after the Resurrection, instructing them about the kingdom of God. His parting words are a commission: "You will receive power when the Holy Spirit has come upon you; and you will be my witnesses in Jerusalem, in all Judea and Samaria, and to the ends of the earth" (Acts 1:8). The vindication of Jesus in the Resurrection leads to the reconstitution of the band of Jesus' followers; in this way a bridge is built from his ministry to theirs—and to ours.

[1] From *Jesus the Jew: A Historian's Reading of the Gospels,* by Geza Vermes (Fortress, 1973); pages 37–41.

10

Christ and the Spirit

Key Concepts:
- What are some central emphases regarding the importance of the Holy Spirit within our Christian tradition?
- In what ways is a discussion of the Holy Spirit integral to our understanding of the nature and work of Jesus Christ?
- What is the significance of the ascension of Jesus for Christology?
- What does the Pentecost story in Acts 2 teach us about the person and work of Jesus?
- What is the relation of Christ and the Spirit in Paul's thought?

In his "Letter to a Roman Catholic," John Wesley articulates what he calls the faith of a "true Protestant" by amplifying the Nicene Creed. As he does so, he identifies what is for those of us in the Wesleyan tradition a key ingredient of the work of the Holy Spirit:

> I believe the infinite and eternal Spirit of God, equal with the Father and the Son, to be not only perfectly holy in himself, but the immediate cause of all holiness in us: enlightening our understandings, rectifying our wills and affections, renewing our natures, uniting our persons to Christ, assuring us of the adoption of sons, leading us in our actions, purifying and sanctifying our souls and bodies to a full and eternal enjoyment of God.[1]

118

Wesley thus attributes directly to the Holy Spirit the ongoing work of renewal, of making those who believe in Christ ever more holy. This is the work of sanctification. It is through the Spirit that Christians are transformed into greater Christlikeness. Becoming like Christ, we reflect more faithfully our vocation as humans to reflect the image of God—the very vocation for which we were first created (Genesis 1:26-27). Charles Wesley invites reflection on these same emphases in his hymn "Spirit of Faith, Come Down":

> Inspire the living faith
>   which whoso'er receive,
> the witness in themselves they have,
>   and consciously believes
> the faith that conquers all,
>   and doth the mountain move,
> and saves whoe'er on Jesus call,
>   and perfects them in love.[2]

Actually, this stanza not only picks up the importance of the work of the Spirit to make believers holy but also accentuates another aspect of the Spirit's activity so important to Methodism. This is the witness of the Spirit, that "inward impression on the soul, whereby the Spirit of God directly witnesses to my spirit, that I am a child of God, that Jesus Christ hath loved me and given Himself for me, and that all my sins are blotted out, and I, even I, am reconciled to God." So wrote John Wesley in his second sermon on "The Witness of the Spirit."[3] Taken together, these two emphases help to secure the importance of the Holy Spirit in the life of believers: to make them more holy and to assure them in their status as God's children.

These two emphases are central for Methodist Christians, but the activity of the Spirit extends more broadly. The daily life of Christians is life led by the Spirit, in which believers are liberated from the rule of sin and death and enabled to live according to the law of love. The Spirit brings Christians in relation to God as his children, inspiring them to recognize God as "Abba, Father." The Spirit enables prayer and fuels hope for the final redemption of all things. The Spirit inspires worship, creates community, empowers believers with spiritual gifts, and produces in them the fruit of the Spirit (see, for example, Romans 8; 12; 1 Corinthians 12–14; Galatians 5).

If we may agree that the Spirit is foundational to Christian existence and maturation, we may still wonder about the relationship of the Spirit to Christology. In what ways is a discussion of the Holy Spirit integral to our understanding of the nature and work of Jesus Christ? This is the focus of the present chapter.

The Spirit of Christ

First Peter 1:10-11 speaks of "the Spirit of Christ" working within the ancient Hebrew prophets. The expression itself is rare in the New Testament, appearing elsewhere only in Romans 8:9. Close parallels are found in Philippians 1:19, where Paul refers to the "Spirit of Jesus Christ," and in Acts 16:7, with Luke's reference to the "Spirit of Jesus." The text in First Peter is particularly interesting, since it indicates that the Spirit at work in the New Testament era is none other than the Spirit of the Lord of whom the Scriptures of Israel speak. That is, the Spirit of Jesus has not ceased to be the Spirit of God; and this has far-reaching implications for Christology.

First, it is worth remembering that the Spirit of Jesus is none other than the Spirit at work in Jesus' life and ministry. Jesus was conceived by the Holy Spirit, anointed with the Holy Spirit, and operated within the arena of the Holy Spirit and with the power of the Holy Spirit. His ministry was thus charismatic in the absolute sense that his very being and activity mediated the Spirit of the Lord to others. Indeed, his own experience of the Spirit encompassed his distinctive humanity and unique relationship to the Father. Inasmuch as the outpouring of the Spirit was integral to Israel's hope of end-time restoration, the presence of the Spirit in and through Jesus' mission was a harbinger of the outpouring of the Spirit on the people of God at Pentecost.

Second, the Holy Spirit is thus said to be poured out

on believers by Jesus Christ. In their own ways, Paul, Luke, and John each declare Jesus to be the Lord of the Spirit, the divine person through whom the Spirit is made available to believers. We will turn to the writings of Luke and Paul below. The Gospel of John has it that, in one of his post-resurrection appearances to his disciples, Jesus "breathed on them and said to them, 'Receive the Holy Spirit'" (20:22). The gift of the Spirit was for them an essential part of their commissioning to carry on the ministry to which Jesus would send them. With direction for the future comes the empowerment of the divine presence: "As the Father has sent me, so I send you" (John 20:21).

What is remarkable about this affirmation of Jesus as Lord of the Spirit is that the Spirit in question never ceases to be the Spirit of God. How is it then that Jesus has the capacity or authority to distribute the Spirit? The only possible answer seems to be that Jesus shares with the Father the lordship of the Spirit, so that the Holy Spirit is understood to extend the presence and work of the risen Lord among his followers. Here is an important witness to Jesus' coregency with God and an affirmation of Jesus' divinity.

Third, the Holy Spirit thus appears as a replacement figure for Jesus. The pages of the New Testament are remarkable for the intimacy they suggest between Christ and his followers; this is to be expected, of course, in the context of the Gospels, with their narration of Jesus' interactions and encounters with people. More noteworthy is the continuation of this sense of familiarity and closeness in the Book of Acts and elsewhere outside of the Gospels. Jesus may not be present in a material sense, but it is clear that Jesus' absence cannot be listed as a distinguishing quality of Christian experience in the New Testament. When people today speak of Jesus as their "friend" or "companion," they bear witness similarly to the difference between Jesus' departure and his absence. How is Jesus present? According to the unanimous testimony of the New Testament, the risen Jesus continues to be actively present through the presence

1.

If the Spirit is the presence of God in the absence of Jesus, how important is it to cultivate "life in the Spirit"? What practices might serve to cultivate that life?

of the Holy Spirit. The relationship of Christ and the Spirit is so forcefully presented, especially in Paul, that the two seem at times virtually to be identified.

The work of the Spirit is thus pivotal for our understanding of the nature and person of Jesus Christ. The Holy Spirit is the basis of Jesus' own relationship to the Father. Jesus the exalted Lord pours out the Spirit on believers and thus bears witness to his exalted status. The presence of the Spirit is the presence of Christ, so that whatever work is attributed to the Spirit—including growth in holiness and assurance of one's relationship to God—may be identified as manifestations of the activity of Christ.

The Ascension of Jesus

The Apostles' Creed reads, "He ascended into heaven, and sitteth at the right hand of God the Father Almighty." Luke is the only New Testament writer to provide an account of the Ascension, and he relates this event in Jesus' career directly to the dispensation of the Holy Spirit at Pentecost. Elsewhere in the New Testament, the Ascension is assumed though not described. Typically, New Testament statements refer to Jesus' exaltation. Sometimes they also refer to its results, Jesus' reign in heaven, often borrowing language from the most quoted Old Testament text in the New Testament, Psalm 110:1:

> The LORD says to my lord,
> "Sit at my right hand
> until I make your enemies your
> footstool."

Luke actually recounts the Ascension of Jesus twice—in the briefest of accounts at the end of his Gospel (Luke 24:50-51) and with slightly more detail at the opening of Acts (1:9-11). The account in Acts has points of contact with other ancient reports of "heavenly journeys" and is especially close to Old Testament and Jewish traditions. In general, such accounts (1) denote the exalted status of the one taken up and (2) reaffirm the relationship of God to his people. Within the Lukan account one easily finds evidence for both these ideas.

Problematic for many people in the modern world is the view of the cosmos that Luke's account seems to portray: "As they were watching, he was lifted up, and a cloud took him out of their sight" (Acts 1:9). What sort of cosmology is this? Does Luke want us to imagine that Jesus kept going up and up and up, until he reached heaven? First, as in Israel's Scriptures, so here the cloud serves to mask Jesus' departure as well as to function as a means of transportation. There is no suggestion in the Lukan text that Jesus' destination could be described simply as "up there." It is worth noting, second, that antiquity knew no *single* cosmology. For example, though antiquity is generally known for its emphasis on a universe centered around the earth, we find evidence that the earth rotated around the sun in the work of the ancient Greek astronomer Aristarchus in the late third century B.C. Not even in ancient Israel can we assume a unified conception of the cosmos, say, with heaven resting on pillars. Our own understanding of the universe continues to unfold; but this does not speak against our capacity to understand that Luke's account is primarily concerned to indicate the exalted status of Jesus, which will later be articulated in terms borrowed from Psalm 110: "at the right hand of God" (Acts 2:33). What is more, with reference to a status-oriented culture like that of the ancient Mediterranean, it is worth reflecting on how better one might portray Jesus' exalted status than in vertical terms.

Luke had written of the necessity of Jesus' ascension already in his Gospel (see Luke 9:31, 51). What is its particular role? Though separated temporally by some forty days, the Resurrection and Ascension are both presented as Jesus' vindication and exaltation. The consequence for Jesus is that, serving as coregent with God, he is able to disseminate beneficently on God's behalf the blessings of salvation (not the least of which is the Holy Spirit).

The Ascension marks Jesus' departure, but not his absence. Accounts of ascension in Second Temple Judaism and in the larger Greco-Roman world typically function to mitigate the sense of divine-human separation, and Luke's is no exception. Within the Book of Acts, Luke weaves the ascension of Jesus into the promise of Jesus' return, the power of "his name" to bring salvation, and the outpouring of the Holy Spirit. In each of these ways, Jesus' ongoing and real presence is guaranteed. For Luke, the Ascension thus carries profound significance for our understanding of the identity and activity of Jesus.

The Pentecostal Outpouring of the Spirit

Luke's narrative of the coming of the Spirit in Acts 2 is Christological in its essential focus. The outpouring of the Holy Spirit at Pentecost authenticates the central Christological claim: Jesus is the enthroned Lord and Christ. This event marks the decisive shift in the history of the actualization of God's promises to his people.

"Pentecost" is shorthand for the festival celebrated on the fiftieth day after Passover, one of the three pilgrim festivals. It is known in Deuteronomy 16:10 as the "festival of weeks." An agricultural festival, Pentecost was the occasion for celebrating the harvest, and particularly for giving thanks to God for his grace in bringing forth fruit from the land. By the first century A.D., the festival had taken on additional meaning. Luke weaves into this particular celebration even more significance.

(1) For example, the Pentecost tradition was now associated with covenant renewal and the anniversary celebration of the giving of the law at Sinai. The coming of the Spirit at Pentecost is thus related to the renewal of the covenant and the reconstitution of the people of God. As interpreted in Joel 2:28-32, this marks the time of Israel's restoration. (2) Luke provides a list of the nations represented among the people gathered at Pentecost in Acts 2:5-11, a list that is reminiscent of the table of nations found in Genesis 10 and the tradition that developed from it throughout the Old Testament and into Second Temple literature. This tradition embodied hopes for the end-time restoration of Israel and for the universal reach of God's salvation. (3) The citation of Joel 2:28-32 in Acts 2:17-21 draws Luke's narrative and the Old Testament Book of Joel together around motifs of fulfillment of the

promise of Israel's restoration, the universalistic impulses of the message of salvation, the threat of judgment, and the call to repent.

(4) Especially interesting is the association of the language-miracle in Acts 2:1-13 with the account of the tower of Babel in Genesis 11:1-9. Generally, those who find an allusion to Babel in Acts 2 regard Luke as portraying a kind of "reversal of Babel"; but a careful reading of Genesis 11 will show that Babel needed no reversal. In fact, the Genesis account does not present the confusion of languages merely as divine punishment. Humanity was to "fill the earth," according to Genesis 1:28; and this mandate was reiterated after the Flood (Genesis 9:1; 10:32). "Scattering," then, is integral to the human vocation—a vocation countered by the unity of language and idolatrous purpose represented by the building project undertaken on the plain of Shinar. In other words, according to Genesis 11, this building program ran counter to God's purpose, first, because it countered his will that humans "fill the earth." Second, the people's plan, "Let us make a name for ourselves" (Genesis 11:4), is evidence of their pride. Third, their plan, articulated in the form of a "Let us" statement, stands in contrast to God's own speech concerning humanity—both in Creation (Genesis 1:26) and in response to this building project (Genesis 11:7): "Let us make humankind . . . Let us go down. . . ." Fourth, the account of the tower of Babel opens with a reference to "one language"— a metaphor for the subjugation and assimilation of conquered peoples by a dominant nation. Thus, although the building project of Genesis 11 is thwarted by God, his scattering the people over all the face of the earth also (and paradoxically) opens fresh possibilities for human community.

How do the phenomena Luke narrates relate to Babel? Acts provides no invitation to return to a single language as a divine promise or blessing. Unity is found, but not by dispensing with distinctions among the peoples. Unity is found, but not by reviving a pre-Babel (imperious) homogeneity. Pentecost does not reverse Babel but parodies it.

With the outpouring of the Spirit, human community is possible, not as a consequence of the presence of a single, all-pervasive, repressive language; not by the dissolution of multiple languages; not, indeed, by the dissolution of all social and national distinctions in the formation of cultural uniformity. This community (or *koinonia*) is rather the consequence of the creative activity of the Spirit who is poured out by Jesus and of the provision of a new rallying point of identity: "in the name of Jesus Christ" (Acts 2:38, 43-47).

All of this and more is the result of Jesus' exaltation to the right hand of God and his pouring out of the gift of the Spirit. The Christological importance of Pentecost reaches still further. What Luke narrates in Acts 2 is no sequence of chance happenings but the work of the God of Israel. Following hard on the heels of reminders of Israel's hopes for restoration, this is a profound and critical affirmation. It demands that Israel's identity be newly constructed in relation to the crucified and exalted Jesus, Lord and Christ, who administers the Holy Spirit. The timeline of the history of the people of God passes through (and not around) this man, Jesus the Nazarene.

What is more, Jesus is Lord of the Spirit and thus is co-regent with God in the beneficent provision of the blessings of salvation. Hence, for Luke the Spirit mediates not only the presence of God the Father but also of Jesus. Though Luke has no Trinitarian theology in the sense that would be developed in subsequent centuries, here, as in the birth narrative of his Gospel, he articulates the status of Jesus in terms that speak of who Jesus is and not simply of what he does.

Finally, Acts 2 advances Luke's presentation of the social arrangement of the believers in the form of an egalitarian community marked by unpretentiousness and the democratization of the experience of the Holy Spirit. Jesus pours out the Spirit; and the Spirit brings about a community of God's people in which the needy receive care, God is worshiped, and no accommodation is made for status-based (whether age-, gender-, or ethnicity-oriented, or some other) factionalism in the economy ushered in by the outpouring of the Holy Spirit (Acts 2:43-47).

2.

Thinking about the relation of the Spirit to our understanding and experience of Christ (and not more broadly of the Spirit's work), what would it mean to describe a person or church as "filled with the Spirit"? What would mark such a church or person?

Paul and the Spirit of Christ

For Paul, the Spirit has the character of Christ; and the Spirit has the role of transforming the hearts and lives of believers so that they embody the dispositions and behaviors of Christ. It would be difficult to overemphasize the importance of this aspect of Paul's thought. Anyone who has attempted to articulate a coherent "theology of the Spirit" from within the Old Testament will realize how vague and diverse conceptions of the Spirit could be in Israel's Scriptures and in later Judaism. In Paul's letters, the apostle speaks with clarity of the Holy Spirit whose being and identity is integrally related to Christ. The Spirit can thus serve as a kind of critical instrument enabling Paul and others to exercise discernment regarding what was genuinely of God and what was not. The Spirit produces love, joy, peace, patience, gentleness, goodness, temperance, meekness, and faith in the lives of those who genuinely follow Christ (see 1 Corinthians 13; Galatians 5:22-23). The Spirit enables believers to confess, "Jesus is Lord" (1 Corinthians 12:3), and leads believers to assurance that they are the children of God (Romans 8:15-16).

The importance of this innovation will become clear below, especially in Chapter 12. In the world in which we live today, all sorts of religious experiences receive their champions; and all put forward their claims to authenticity. As long as the identity of the Spirit or the notion of spiritual experience resides in the land of the indeterminate and vague, arbitration between competing claims is not only difficult but probably also indefensible. When the identity and nature of the Holy Spirit is specifically tied to Christ, however, when "to walk according to the Spirit" is equated with life "in Christ," then the church does possess a means of critical evaluation. Accordingly, only those experiences and affirmations that manifest the Spirit as the Spirit of Christ Jesus are to be recognized and embraced.

From time to time in the Pauline writings, the Spirit and Christ seem to be interchangeable, as if they were the same being altogether. This is truest in Romans 8:9-11, where

3,

Sometimes Christians struggle to discern the voice of the Spirit in the hubbub of other voices. How might our appreciation of the identity of the Spirit as the Spirit of Jesus Christ assist us in our hearing?

the phrases "the Spirit of God," "the Spirit of Christ," and "Christ . . . in you" refer to the same reality. However, in the expression "Spirit of Christ," Spirit and Christ are not equated. For example, the Spirit is not said to have had a material existence or human nature; the Spirit did not die for us, was not raised from the dead, and so on. The Spirit does come upon believers as a consequence of faith in Christ, however; and it is unthinkable that a believer in Christ would not have the Spirit (Romans 8:9).

Christians are therefore known as those in whom the Spirit is manifesting the character of Christ and in whom the Spirit is inspiring the confession that Jesus is Lord. The Spirit mediates to believers their newly found relationship to the Father, just as the Spirit binds together all believers into a single communion of the Spirit, the body of Christ. And the Spirit inspires, empowers, and directs Christian worship and *koinonia*. In these ways the Spirit makes present to believers the person and ministry of Jesus of Nazareth, who died and was raised.

[1] From "Letter to a Roman Catholic," by John Wesley, in *John Wesley,* edited by Albert C. Outler, Library of Protestant Thought (Oxford University Press, 1964); page 495.

[2] From "Spirit of Faith, Come Down," in *The United Methodist Hymnal* (Copyright © 1989 The United Mehodist Publishing House); 332.

[3] From "The Witness of the Spirit," by John Wesley, in *Sermons on Several Occasions* (Epworth, 1944); page 115.

11

Return in Glory

Key Concepts:

- What are the four primary images used in Scripture to describe the end, and what do they each emphasize?
- When the New Testament writings speak of Jesus' return, what are their two primary emphases?
- Who or what is the "antichrist"?
- When we pray, "Thy kingdom come," for what are we praying?

This is not all there is. With this statement we reach the bedrock of Christian faith. We believe that, in Creation, God instigated a reality that has yet fully to be realized; that the consummation of God's purpose lies in the future, outside of time as we know it; and that God's project will reach its completion with the return of Christ. To state it negatively, without an authentic fulfillment of God's purpose for humankind and the whole cosmos in the future, his purpose in the present loses its point. For this reason, the return of Christ is integral to our understanding of God's will and is a crucial milestone in our understanding of Jesus' person and work. There is an important sense, then, in which the "journey of Christology" of which we spoke in Chapter 1 continues—both for Jesus and for those who follow him—until his return.

The return of Christ, which is the focus of this chapter, has

1.

Complete this sentence: "When I hear people talking about the end, I _____." Please explain.

long been a troublesome subject. Undoubtedly, an important aspect of the hostility Jesus encountered had to do with the fact that his message and ministry did not mesh well with expectations of the divine rule in his day. Jesus declared the advent of the kingdom of God, but the realities of life in Palestine did not seem to reflect God's dominion. Our God reigns? Here? Jesus addressed those questions in two different ways. First, in parables he remarked that those who look for the Kingdom in the wrong ways and in the wrong places are likely to miss its presence. The kingdom of God is like a mustard seed, he insisted, not like a mighty oak tree. Second, he spoke of the day of the Lord, still to come, and of his own return to bring history to its divinely purposed goal. God's project would be actualized in a series of events, some of which were already occurring, the last of which would be the return of Jesus.

The subject of the return of Christ continues to be troubling today. On the one hand, this is because some Christians are embarrassed by the fanaticism that often accompanies end-time thinking. Some people, it seems, spend too much time thinking about the end! And in recent decades a veritable industry has arisen in support of end-time speculation and end-time fears. On the other hand, some Christians think too little of the end. Those who are trying to make a name for themselves in the world and to fit into its designs are not likely to nurture hope for a messianic kingdom that will transform and renew everything. Civil religion, from the time of the Roman Empire up to present-day America, is more likely to quash end-time hopes than to support them. Church institutions sometimes find themselves doing the same in order to recommend themselves as representing fully God's interests on earth. But the Christian hope in the consummation of God's purpose, with its expectation of a "new heaven and a new earth," blunts all parodies of the kingdom of God.

To Judge the Quick and the Dead

The Apostles' Creed, which has been the primary confession of the church in the West, speaks of Jesus' return in these words: "From thence he shall come to judge the quick and the dead," that is, both those who are living and those who have already died. Although this emphasis on judgment is important, this is nonetheless an unfortunately one-sided way of representing the return of Christ. In a culture like ours, where guilt plays so pivotal a role, the image of "Christ the Judge" often evokes responses of fear rather than of hope. We would do well to remember, then, that the purpose of Christ is also to bring renewal, to set things right, to establish a never-ending kingdom of peace and righteousness.

Of course, with regard to the image of judgment, it is also worth remembering who the agent of justice is. For end-time renewal to come, justice must be exercised; but this is the justice of the one who "came not to be served but to serve and to give his life a ransom for many." The one whose obedience to God and love for humanity took him to the cross is the one who brings judgment, and he will judge according to his own message. Indeed, Christ is himself the basis of judgment. Who has open arms toward Jesus and his message? Who has welcomed the gospel in faith? Who has joined with Jesus in the service of the kingdom of God? Here is the criterion of judgment.

Images of Apocalyptic

Presentations of the return of Jesus and other related end-time events borrow heavily from apocalyptic thought that flowered in Second Temple Judaism. "Apocalyptic" categories are not always familiar to us, reared in other times and places. In fact, the apocalyptic literature found in and outside the Old and New Testaments, especially the books of Daniel and Revelation, are replete with images, sometimes this-worldly, often quite fantastic. In an important sense, the language of apocalyptic was the language of word-pictures. This was due to the environment within which apocalyptic was born and nurtured. Apocalyptic was grounded in the social experience of powerlessness and marginalization and in the conviction that Israel's destiny would never be fulfilled within this world but would come in the next as a consequence of God's direct intervention. By means of the imagination, God's people turned to apocalyptic in order to see through the lens of faith what was beyond the horizon of the unaided human eye. The ambiguities of present history could make sense when portrayed on the greater mural of God's dealings in history and beyond history, on the earth and in the world of the supernatural.

Apocalyptic images of the future congregated around a series of motifs: (1) the immediacy of the end, (2) the cataclysmic character of the end, (3) the transformation of the cosmos, and (4) divine provision in the new epoch of salvation.

(1) **The Immediacy of the End:** In the New Testament, the immediacy of the end is conveyed in a variety of images, including the thief who comes in the night (for example, Matthew 24:43; 1 Thessalonians 5:2), the master who returns after a long journey (Mark 13:34-36; Luke 12:35-38, 41-48), and the bridegroom who arrives in the middle of the night (Matthew 25:1-13). Additionally, lists of events or historical records could serve this purpose. In Daniel, for example, as in Revelation, almost all the events that were to have happened before the end had already occurred when the book was first written. Similarly, in Mark 13, the events that would precede the end are plainly characteristic of most every age. These timetables insinuate strongly that the end is imminent.

(2) **The Cataclysmic Character of the End:** Most apocalyptic texts that warn of the end of the world do so with reference to a stereotyped list of catastrophes expected to precede the Final Judgment. These include famine, earthquakes, wars, betrayal, signs in the heavens, and so on (for example, Joel 2; Mark 13; Revelation). The apocalyptic discourse in Mark 13 also speaks of the destruction of the Jerusalem Temple as a sign of the end, due no doubt to the centrality of the Temple in defining the world of the Jewish people. Some writings also speak of the coming of a time of great tribulation (for example, Daniel 12:1; Mark 13:24; Revelation 7:14), an unprecedented time of affliction numbered among the many woes that accompany the

end. Second Peter 3:10 summarizes this idea: "The heavens will pass away with a loud noise, and the elements will be dissolved with fire, and the earth and everything that is done on it will be disclosed" (or "burned up"; see footnote *y*). These images underscore the power of evil and the need for faithful, holy living. Human efforts will never suffice to overcome the forces of evil. Only God can do so; and this he will do, at the end of time. The present is the arena for constant readiness and fidelity.

(3) **The Transformation of the Cosmos:** Second Peter also summarizes well the apocalyptic vision of reversal at the end. True, the destruction of the heavens and the earth will be complete; "but . . . we wait for new heavens and a new earth, where righteousness is at home" (3:13). John uses similar symbolism (Revelation 21), drawing explicit attention to the absence of death, mourning, crying, and pain; "for the first things have passed away" (Revelation 21:4; compare, for example, Isaiah 33:24; 65:20). Nor, John adds, will the new earth include any "sea" (Revelation 21:1)—a reference to the final triumph over evil, symbolized by the powers of chaos represented in the sea and the sea monster: the Dragon/dragons (Job 7:12; Psalm 74:13), Behemoth/Leviathan (Job 40:15-24; Psalm 74:13-14; 104:26; Isaiah 27:1), Rahab (Job 9:13; Psalm 89:10), and the serpent (Job 26:13).

Paul uses apocalyptic imagery to denote the transformation already overtaking creation "in Christ" when he remarks, "If anyone is in Christ, there is a new creation" (2 Corinthians 5:17). This assertion is often mistranslated so as to affirm that "he [or she] is a new creation" (for example, the New International Version), as though God's redemptive work were subjective and individualistic rather than cosmological and eschatological. Paul's point is that "in Christ" old things are already passing away, and new things have come.

Cosmic transformation is also visualized in the judgment that accompanies the end of the world, but even here one recognizes an important twist. Apocalyptic literature was keen in its anticipation of judgment, promising salvation and life for those who are part of the marginalized com-

munity and damnation for those who are among the powerful. In employing the apocalyptic image of the end-time
banquet scene, however, Jesus notes that people will come
not simply from a chosen remnant of the faithful, but from
the four corners of the earth to enjoy fellowship in the
kingdom of God (Luke 13:29). What is more, restoration
is not reserved for humanity but is for all creation (Romans
8:19-22; Ephesians 1:9-10; Colossians 1:15-20).

(4) **Divine Provision in the New Epoch of Salvation:**
The apocalyptic vision is not all one of doom and gloom.
It is true that apocalyptic writers express little hope for the
recovery of the world in its present form, but this does not
keep them from believing that God will bring "times of
refreshing" (Acts 3:20) or that God is nevertheless working
in the present world to bring his purposes to completion.
God will provide for his people, though the shape of that
provision is often context specific. To people experiencing
economic oppression or deprivation, God's provision might
take the form of streets of gold (Revelation). To the hungry
or to those who long for restored fellowship with God, the
heavenly feast, provided and hosted by God, is an apt symbol of restoration (for example, Isaiah 25:6; Luke 14:15;
Revelation 19:9).

Images of Jesus' Return

In Christian art, representations of the Second Coming
have generally developed along two lines. The more popular portrays Jesus in his role at the Great Judgment, following his return. The second has Jesus returning to earth on
the clouds, accompanied by an army of angels. This latter
image borrows from Jesus' own comments (for example,
Mark 13:26; 14:62). Viewed together, these images display
the two primary emphases of New Testament presentations
of the Second Coming—its certainty and suddenness on
the one hand, the need for vigilant preparedness on the
other.

As we have noted, the sudden and unexpected nature of
Jesus' return is captured in the image of the thief who
comes in the night or the bridegroom who arrives in the

middle of the night. In these examples, "darkness" plays an obvious role. This is due both to the tendency to relate light/dark by analogy to God/Satan (for example, Acts 26:18; Colossians 1:13) and to the normal rhythm of life that has us active during the day, sleeping during the night (compare Mark 4:26-27). While highlighting the abruptness of the Second Coming, then, these images also underscore the necessity of constant readiness, symbolized in the call to stay awake.

This dual emphasis, surprise and readiness, inspired the biblical writers sometimes to mix (or at least to develop) related metaphors. For example, Jesus is coming like a thief; so his followers should keep their clothes on (Revelation 16:15). Being clothed in this instance has to do with constant faithfulness in the midst of hardship or suffering, similar to that demonstrated by Jesus in his suffering and death. Paul, on the other hand, could develop the metaphor in the other direction, insisting that Christians, who live in the light, should resist behavior characteristic of the night—such as drunkenness (1 Thessalonians 5:1-8; see also Romans 13:11-14).

In describing the second coming of Jesus, Paul uses another cluster of images borrowed from the triumph of the divine warrior. The trumpet call (1 Corinthians 15:52; 1 Thessalonians 4:16), for example, is reminiscent of the call to battle, just as the picture of the faithful meeting the Lord in the air (1 Thessalonians 4:17) is drawn from the practice of coming out of the city to welcome the returning warrior who has been successful in battle. The use of this cluster of images communicates that Jesus is God's agent of salvation but also defines salvation, in part, as the defeat of Satan (and all that would oppose God's purpose) in cosmic warfare. The Book of Revelation, of course, continues the theme of divine warfare in relation to Jesus' return.

What is telling about Revelation's portrayal of the cosmic struggle is its pervasive portrayal of Jesus as the Lamb who defeats evil. This suggests that the overturning of evil at the Second Coming will not be accomplished by force or power—at least, not as "power" is usually defined. Instead,

2.

Biblical discussion regarding the return of Jesus invites us to live our present lives in light of the future. In practical terms, what might this look like?

evil will be overcome then, just as it is now, through faithful service that refuses worldly ways of power and might. According to Luke, Jesus himself spoke of his return along these lines: The master who returns "will fasten his belt and have [the faithful] sit down to eat, and he will come and serve them" (12:37).

What of the Antichrist?

Many Christians today and in every generation since the coming of Christ have concerned themselves with the identity of the antichrist. This is due in part to the specific warning of Jesus that "false messiahs and false prophets will appear and produce signs and omens, to lead astray, if possible, the elect" (Mark 13:22).

This concern is far older than the first century, however. From its earliest days, Israel was interested in distinguishing God's genuine messengers from those who only pretended to represent God. For example, in Deuteronomy 18:21-22, the question is raised, "How can we recognize a word that the LORD has not spoken?" Moses replied that the truth of a prophetic word depends on whether it happens, whether it proves true. Passages in the New Testament, too, emphasize the need to distinguish God's message from its counterfeits. First John 4:1-3 warns that false prophets have gone out into the world. These people are false teachers who deny the Father and the Son (1 John 2:22) and refuse to accept that Jesus really came to earth as a human (1 John 4:2-3; see 2 John 7). Such people speak by "the spirit of the antichrist" (1 John 4:3).

The word *antichrist* itself is rare in the New Testament and absent in the Old Testament. Other words are used for this figure, however. Jesus spoke of "false Messiahs" (Mark 13:22) as persons who will appear in the period before the end. Unlike Jesus, such persons will use their powers to show off, to prove that they are sent by God. But their real aim is to lead people away from God. The antichrist is like these "false Christs," except he may even require that people worship him as though he were a god. Paul does not use the term *antichrist*, but in 2 Thessalonians 2:3-4 he mentions the "lawless one." This person will claim to be God while opposing everything that God stands for. He is the very embodiment of evil.

Revelation 13 describes the "beast rising out of the sea" (13:1) as the antichrist. It does not do this by using the term *antichrist* but by portraying the beast as Satan's forgery of the authentic Christ, Jesus the Lamb of God. The beast of the sea in Revelation 13 is Satan's agent to make war against God's people. This description is given in such detail to emphasize the depth of its evil. As one who tries to seize our worship, our loyalty, our obedience, the beast is a counterfeit Christ.

The term *antichrist* appears only in First and Second John. There, John not only prophesies the coming of the antichrist (2 John 2:7) but also goes on to say that antichrists have already arrived and are now at work among God's people (1 John 2:18-19). They are false teachers, people who refuse to accept that Jesus is the authentic Christ. They do not understand who God is, so their relations with others do not exhibit God's love; and their actions are immoral. They even separate themselves from God's people. For John, the presence of these antichrists signifies that "the last days" are already present.

Clearly, concerns about the antichrist can never be relegated simply to discussions about the end. Instead, these passages demonstrate the constant challenge for the people of God to be on the alert. The enemies of Christ, those who oppose the purposes of God, are not to be expected simply at some future time, just before the end. They are already at work. What is more, they present themselves in subtle ways, beckoning to Christians with showy signs of power. They seem to be from God. They proclaim a message that we want to hear: peace, pleasure, prosperity. But in doing so, they work to entrap us in thoughts and lifestyles that actually work against God's purpose.

3.

If the phenomenon of the "antichrist" is already present in the world, how do we recognize it? Could it be that some of our own dispositions betray the influence of the antichrist? Please explain.

What Sort of "End"?

When we pray, "Thy kingdom come," for what are we actually praying? Did Jesus and his contemporaries really anticipate a finale to this world and this history and the opening of a new form of existence? Should we expect an end to time and space as we know it?

These questions arise today from a number of sources, the most forceful being the Jesus Seminar. Members of the Seminar, we may recall, met regularly in the 1980's and 1990's to determine what, if anything, in the Gospels Jesus actually said. In one of its more sensational moves, the Seminar voted overwhelmingly that Jesus did not expect the end. What Jesus and his contemporaries expected, and what we should work toward, is not a personal return of Jesus, but the blossoming of a world in which the values and orientations of Jesus are shared by all. "End" has to do with "aim," not with "finish."

On this point, members of the Jesus Seminar have a handle on an important reality. When we compare Jesus' words about the end of the ages with similar material from apocalyptic writers of his era, we see the remarkable restraint he exercised. At times, some Jewish writers seem in their writings almost to distribute calendars with "The End" clearly marked. According to Mark 13, when Jesus' disciples inquired about the time of the end, Jesus adopted a different strategy. He admitted that "about that day or hour no one knows, neither the angels in heaven, nor the Son, but only the Father" (13:32). What is more, he peppered his reply with encouragement to watch: "Beware" (Mark 13:5, 9), "Be alert" (13:23), "Keep alert" (13:33), "Keep awake" (13:35, 37). Evidently, faithful discipleship was central to Jesus' end-time concerns, far more so than providing a calendar by which to determine the end of time.

Hence, in this case, the perspective of the Jesus Seminar coheres well with an important emphasis in the Gospel accounts of Jesus. This is that Jesus encouraged faithful discipleship by which his followers would not give themselves to end-time speculation but to serving the purposes of God and embodying God's own concerns for the world. "Thy kingdom come!" is, at least in part, a prayer by which we commit ourselves to aligning ourselves with God's own purposes in the world and participating fully in acts of holy love.

But this is not the end of the story. And, indeed, it is not a story of final justice and reconciliation; for it does not address the travesties of our human past. In the wake of the almost unspeakable national and international calamities of slavery, apartheid, and ethnic cleansing, is it possible to believe in a just God who does not in the end set things right? As Paul insisted, "if for this life only we have hoped in Christ, we are of all people most to be pitied" (1 Corinthians 15:19).

The kingdom of God is not only a "world view." The kingdom of God is not a reality that we can implement by means of our own efforts. The kingdom is God's. It is the active rule of God, a reality that is already breaking into the world but is not yet fully realized. Around us we continue to see and experience the power of evil. Injustice abounds. Relationships are not pervaded by love. Violence continues—sometimes, it seems, unabated. God, who acted in history in Jesus, has demonstrated his loving, redemptive purpose. He continues to act so as to bring that purpose to its realization, and he will bring his saving purpose to completion at the end of history by the return of his Son.

Christ will be revealed as Savior and Judge to all humanity and will establish once and for all the eternal kingdom that will transcend space and time as we experience them today. In this way the second coming of Christ will embrace all that is past; set right what is wrong; and introduce the new order, transforming heaven and earth. This is the public and triumphant vindication of God and all those who have suffered unjustly for the sake of God's purposes. It is love's victory.

12

Jesus, Lord of All

Key Concepts:

- What are some of the ways in which Jesus is understood on the continent of Africa? Asia? South America?
- What are the three primary positions people have taken in discussing the relation of Jesus Christ to the world's religions?
- What are some of the ways in which we might learn from and participate with persons of other faiths?
- What significance does the Christian affirmation of Jesus Christ as the ultimate expression of God's self-disclosure have for our understanding of Christian mission today?

The question "Who is Jesus?" resists simple answers. The New Testament itself provides no single, definitive answer but instead employs a wide range of images: Son of God, Lord, Messiah, Servant, Living Stone, Lamb, Logos, and many more. No two images are exactly alike, nor can they be simply equated. Each points to some important aspect of Jesus' person and work, but none is capable of capturing who Jesus is fully or for all people. For this reason, when Anglican Bishop Stephen Neill wrote his introduction to the message of the New Testament, he called it *Jesus Through Many Eyes* (1976).

Looked at through different eyes in different times and places, the significance of Jesus appears differently. In part, this is a result of the depth of Jesus' importance to the whole world and in God's purpose. Every image reveals certain aspects of

Jesus while concealing others; and the wealth of his significance requires that an abundance of titles be used, images be painted, and stories be told concerning him if we are to understand him even partially. This is also because different people, drawing on their own experiences, understand his significance differently. "Son of Man" may work well enough to describe Jesus in an ancient Palestinian context; but the term finds little traffic in Paul's Christology, which was developed in and for urban centers outside the land of the Jews.

In the Acts of the Apostles, Luke reports that in a decisive moment of insight, Peter came to the realization that "Jesus Christ . . . is Lord of all" (Acts 10:36). The importance of this moment is registered in the fact that it occurred in the home of Cornelius, a Gentile known for his piety but who was nonetheless neither a Jew nor even a Jewish convert. The church in Jerusalem had been clear that Jesus is Lord and that through him the divine blessings of salvation are available; but up to this point in the narrative of Acts, Peter and his fellow apostles had limited their missionary interaction almost solely to the Jewish people. Against the backdrop of a vision from God and upon hearing Cornelius' own testimony of how God had spoken to him through an angel, Peter experienced a breakthrough. The story of Jesus has implications outside of Judea! And Peter proceeded to proclaim the good news in such a way that began to address the relevance of Jesus for other places.

What does it mean today to affirm and proclaim that Jesus is Lord of all? This is the focus of this chapter, which has two primary concerns. The first has to do with images of Jesus in other places in the world. What might we learn about Jesus from our Christian sisters and brothers around the globe? How is the lordship of Jesus being expressed in the world's churches? The second has to do with the scandal of our understanding of Jesus as Lord of all. What is the relationship between Jesus' universal lordship and the reality of religious pluralism in the world today? In a world populated by persons who embrace one of the world's major religions (Judaism, Hinduism, Buddhism, Islam) or some other, what does it mean to affirm with Paul that there is "one God" and "one Lord" (1 Corinthians 8:6)?

Global Images of Jesus

Who is Jesus in Africa? in South America? in Asia? For some of us, the questions themselves are troublesome. After all, is it not true that "Jesus Christ is the same yesterday and today and forever" (Hebrews 13:8)? How, then, could Jesus have one face in Africa, another in South America? Why would we imagine that Jesus would be regarded differently in Korea than in the Midwest of the United States? Our answer to this question comes in two parts. First, although Jesus is the same yesterday, today, and forever, our knowledge and experience of him are not static. As we grow in our own discipleship and in relationship to Christ, our understanding of him changes; and we think of him in fresh or renewed ways. Second, the language and metaphors by which we speak of Jesus will change as we move from one people to the next (or even from one generation to the next). None of our language is sufficient to apprehend the totality of Jesus' person and work, and we understand him only in part. For this reason, not only might we expect different peoples to picture Jesus in different ways, but we are well advised to learn from those different peoples how they see Jesus. Their perceptions of Jesus, their understandings of discipleship, may help to fill out our own. What is more, theirs may indicate to us those areas in which our perspectives on the faith are parochial and self-serving and in need of enlarging.

Are all images of Jesus equally valid? Of course not. This is true for portraits of Christ that arise in Indonesia as much as for those that arise in Indiana, however. This is because we regard Scripture as the canon by which we measure the validity of any witness about Christ. This fact does not mean that our images of Jesus must derive directly from the pages of Scripture, however. The diversity of representations of Jesus' person and work within Scripture already authorizes the development of fresh images by which to articulate his importance to us. It does mean that we bring our attempts at naming the name of Jesus in different cultural settings back to the text of Scripture in order to measure the degree to which they cohere with the witness of the Bible. What does this image reveal of Jesus? What does it conceal? These are questions to which the community of Jesus' followers must continually return as we struggle to be faithful in our witness to Christ.

Christ in Africa

The question "Who is Jesus in Africa?" is, of course, hopelessly vague. Africa is a continent of gargantuan proportions, with a lively, creative, and growing Christian movement; and we cannot hope to represent the whole of the African Christian movement here. We can, however, speak at a certain level of abstraction of Christological images that have had importance within Africa. One of these would be the portrait of **Christ as Victor**. Jesus is the one who overcomes the powers of evil, the devil, disease, hatred, and death. Why this image is relevant rests in the presence of a traditional culture in which people are cognizant of a full range of powers operative in the world: spirits, magic, witchcraft, and more.

It is interesting that African Christians are able to find in the Gospels a measure of solidarity with Jesus that people in the West might overlook. Matthew and Luke particularly represent Jesus' life in ways that reflect the rites of passage by which a child is incorporated into society: birth, circumcision (or its cultural equivalent), and initiation into adulthood. For African Christians, too, Jesus' genealogies are important for establishing his identity and status among his people. His death serves also to demonstrate his solidarity with humanity. In some important ways, then, the African Christian has more direct access to the Gospel portraits than we in the West, since the cultures of the ancient Mediterranean and of Africa intersect at numerous points.

Another African image is **Christ as Ancestor**. The strength of this image derives from a view of the world alive with powers at work in all aspects of existence. These powers uphold and sustain the order of the cosmos and can be deployed for good and evil. The ancestors mediate to the community its identity and structure and facilitate its health and happiness. How Jesus relates to the importance

1.

Have you had an intercultural encounter with someone that caused you to understand Jesus in a fresh way: If so, please describe it. If not, consider planning opportunities for interaction and worship with representatives of other cultures—perhaps international students from a local college or university or persons of socioeconomic and/or racial backgrounds different from your own.

of the ancestors varies. Some regard him as the great or greatest ancestor, superior to the others on account of his incomparable closeness to God. Accordingly, Jesus' standards of moral and corporate behavior are to be followed in every aspect of life, with the result that justice is served.

In the African Christian context, Jesus is also known as **Healer**. Drawing on the importance of the role of the traditional medicine man, Jesus is portrayed as the source of power to heal and to cast out demonic spirits.

Christ in Asia

In the past two centuries, theologians in the West have struggled especially with questions of history, particularly with how to make sense of the historical Jesus. The importance of Jesus' humanity and the relation of that humanity to God's work in a specific history have been at the heart of discussion. What we tend to regard as central becomes quite problematic on Asian soil, not least in countries such as India where Hinduism has had far-reaching influence. Hinduism emphasizes the unity of all life; the question therefore arises whether Christology can address the unity of life that embraces the historical as well as nature and consciousness. In more general terms, how can the particularity of the coming of Jesus in space and time be understood in transcendent terms that make sense of Christ in his universality and eternality?

Of course, the New Testament is not devoid of this concern. Jesus is presented as the agent of Creation in John's Gospel; and in Colossians, Paul presents Jesus in cosmic terms that embrace not only embodied life but also transcendent powers. We read in Indian theologians, however, that these images need further emphasis and elaboration. "Christ," in a sense, must be understood theologically as encompassing more than the historical person Jesus of Nazareth.

Asian theologians more influenced by Taoism emphasize categories of transcendence as well and embrace such images as **Christ as Word, Christ as Light,** and the **Cosmic Christ**. These images are dynamic and emphasize the creative role of Christ in revelation. Christ's redemptive work opens us to a greater reality and to harmony with all. He is the center of the inner person as well as the axis of human life.

Christ in Latin America

Questions about Jesus Christ take on a radically different character in Latin America. This is partially due to the historical events by which the church came to Latin America through the agency of Spanish conquistadors and partially due to the experience of poverty and conflict that has characterized so much of its history more recently.

When the Spanish came to what we today call South America, they brought with them two images of the adult Christ: the suffering Jesus who remained passive in the midst of his passion as an expression of his submission to his destiny before God and the royal, conquering Christ who reigns over his kingdom. This suffering Jesus was the image with which the native peoples were to identity, while the image of the conquering Christ belonged to those conquistadors who brought Christian faith and Spanish rule to the Aztecs, Mayas, and Incas. Not without good reason, then, Latin American theologians have felt an urgent need to examine critically the traditional images of Christ that have formed the basis of Christian mission.

As before, we can paint only with the broadest of strokes. Two primary images come to mind. One is the Christ of Latin American theologians, for whom the prophetic but suffering figure of Jesus is paramount. This is the Jesus who identified with the poor, both in his own life and in his teaching. In order to understand Scripture, Jesus demonstrates, the church must likewise declare its solidarity with and work actively on behalf of the poor. We understand Christ only as we follow him in the prophetic ministry of cultivating justice in the real world of those who suffer.

From our perspective in the northern hemisphere, we might imagine that this portrait of Jesus would be comforting and helpful to those who live in what is often referred to as the "dark belly of the underdeveloped world." The reality of Christian existence is quite different for many who live in the villages and barrios of Latin America.

Rather than embracing a Jesus who will meet them in their marginality and fear of shame, many attend churches where Christ is said to offer them escape from their painful worlds. The cross of Christ is for them not so much the ultimate way in which God shows his concern for and union with human suffering. According to this way of thinking, the cross of Christ addresses our relationships with God, but not the context of our lives. Reconciliation within the human family or with the larger world of nature is not on the agenda of the gospel. In his resurrection, Christ helps us to transcend our world of despair—at least during the hours in which we are in church. This disembodied Christology is not indigenous to Latin America but, sadly, is an export from the United States.

Some Reflections

Even a cursory discussion like this one can point in provocative directions. Most importantly, we have suggested that our images of Christ have roots in the worlds in which we live. This should not surprise us, since it is precisely in our worlds that Christ comes to us to reveal himself to us, to bring us hope, and to challenge us to faithfulness before God. How we understand reality, how we understand and articulate our deepest needs—answers to these and related issues help to shape how we hear the hope and call of the gospel.

It is also true, of course, that our understanding of even our own realities is always only partial. Christ addresses us where we are, to be sure, but also helps us to see better than we could before the nature of our worlds and, thus, the nature of our needs. The question is, "Will we allow him to open our eyes to these needs, or will we turn a blind eye to them?" One of the ways in which our understanding of the nature and work of Jesus is challenged and expanded is in conversation with our Christian brothers and sisters around the globe. They may see what we do not. They may see what we refuse to see. They may lead us into a fuller understanding of Christ.

2.

How is your church presently engaged in serving and proclaiming the universal lordship of Jesus? What does it mean in your community to say, "Jesus is Lord of all"?

Christ and the World's Religions

The Christian missionary movement has always had to struggle with how Jesus relates to other religions, whether that means one of the world religions (Islam, Judaism, Hinduism, Buddhism) or more traditional and/or local religions. Increasingly today in the United States, questions of this nature have both relevance and urgency. Immigration has brought the world's religions into our worlds; and, increasingly, people in our own neighborhoods experiment with or embrace new religions. In such a world, is it really true, as John's Gospel reports, that Jesus is the way, the truth, and the life, that no one comes to the Father except through Jesus (John 14:6)? Is it really true, as the Book of Acts has it, that there is salvation in no one other than Jesus Christ of Nazareth, that no other name has been given by which we must be saved (Acts 4:12)? In the context of the realities we face, a range of positions has been generated, from "exclusivism" to "inclusivism" to "pluralism." After reviewing these briefly, we will conclude with a series of important landmarks in the discussion.

The traditional view of **exclusivism** claims that Jesus Christ is the only source of human salvation and that salvation requires an explicit confession of faith in him. Some who hold to this position allow for some form of continuity between one's awareness of God through a non-Christian religion and one's encounter with Jesus at or after death. **Inclusivism** also claims that Jesus is salvation's only source but maintains that explicit confession of faith in him is not always necessary for salvation. Some can be saved by responding positively to their deepest awareness of God, an awareness that might come through practice of another religion. This does not locate salvation in human effort or insight. Rather, God initiates and sustains the process through means such as prevenient grace (especially in the Wesleyan tradition) or the universal working of Christ.

Pluralism, on the other hand, regards Christian claims to the uniqueness of Christ as imperialistic. Other names may be redemptive, and the uniqueness and ultimacy of

Jesus are not essential to Christian belief. Accordingly, what is needed is not missionary work and evangelism but dialogue, which should lead to common commitments and actions. Indeed, for some pluralists, what is essential to Christian faith is found in other religions as well.

Landmarks in the Discussion

What are we to make of this discussion? How do we respond constructively? Let me offer the following comments for orientation.

Belief that Jesus is Lord of all should not lead us to imagine that the grace of God is found only in Christianity. Within the Wesleyan tradition, we are convinced that God's grace knows no frontiers and can work preveniently in ways both known and unknown.

Belief that Jesus is Lord of all should not lead us to imagine that Christianity monopolizes the truth. The sanctity of life, for example, concern for the needy, and love for one's neighbor can be found in many other religions and are practiced among those who claim no religion at all. In fact, it is sometimes true that gazing into the mirror of other religions reminds us of aspects of our own faith that we have forgotten or overlooked.

Belief that Jesus is Lord of all should encourage our growth in wisdom and discernment as we seek to understand the presence of Jesus in other cultures. Christians sometimes worry about the ways in which the message and person of Jesus are meaningful in other cultures simply because language and images are used that are alien to our experience of him.

We should look with suspicion on all claims that the substance of Buddhism is found in Christianity or that Hinduism's main concerns are shared by Christianity and so on. The major world religions, including Christianity, are not patterns of mountains and valleys waiting to be leveled. Although we may compare the Christian idea of God with the Buddhist idea, we cannot forget that the Buddhist idea of God is inexorably connected to a whole system of beliefs and practices that are Buddhist and not Christian (and vice versa). The law of retribution that determines one's life and fate in this world is alien to Christian faith;

but it is questionable whether one could, for the sake of religious pluralism, deny this law and call oneself a Hindu. In the same way, if for classical Christian faith Jesus is the ultimate revelation of the nature of God, then we cannot deny that ultimacy *and* embrace Christian faith.

Christian faith rests on the bedrock of the affirmation of Jesus' unique relationship to God—indeed, his deity. Scripture represents salvation as an act that only a divine agent could bring. Even if something of God is known in many religions, which we need not deny, it is only with the resurrection of Jesus that God "commands all people everywhere to repent" (Acts 17:30-31).

Of course, it is true that biblical language about Jesus is metaphorical; but this is not to say that other metaphors are equally expressive of God's self-disclosure. Scripture uses a range of metaphors because no one can define Jesus *fully*. This is not to say that they cannot describe some aspects of him *truly*, however.

We have seen that the Spirit through whom God's presence and purpose is known in the world is the Spirit of Jesus Christ. This places boundaries around what experiences, religious or otherwise, can legitimately be named as experiences of the God we know in Jesus Christ. The "Spirit" has in recent decades of religious discussion become an amorphous category for affirming the presence of God in unexpected ways or surprising contexts. Such talk, however, must be tamed with reference to scriptural witness to the self-disclosure of God in Jesus Christ.

All religious claims, even those put forward by pluralists, are exclusive in some sense. Those who seek to find common or universal truth in all religions can do so only by according privilege to one idea or set of ideas and dismissing others. While rejecting Christian affirmations of Jesus' unique universality, pluralists must presuppose others. For example, it is common today to insist that all religions have as their common ground the pursuit of human liberation and wholeness. What are we to make of the fact that different religions look differently on the meaning of "humanity"? Who defines "liberation"? "Wholeness"? Among Christians, of course, these concepts take their meaning above all from the revelation of God the Creator and Savior, known ultimately in the mission of God's Son, Jesus. Other religions will have their own perspectives on these pivotal questions.

We cannot deny, however, that claims like "Jesus is Lord" have often served in oppressive ways, especially when they have been tethered to imperialistic claims, ancient (for example, the "Crusades" of the medieval period) or contemporary (for example, the importation of Western values with Christian faith in the missionary movements of the nineteenth and twentieth centuries). At such points, however, the problem lies not with the affirmation itself, but with the failure of those making it to discern its substance on biblical grounds. The lordship of Jesus is not realized or recognized in coercion; indeed, his lordship is set over against all oppressive rulers, belief systems, and values (see, for example, Luke 22:24-27; Philippians 2:6-11).

Jesus is necessary for salvation. Can only those who know about him and confess him explicitly be saved? In the end, of course, this is a question that only God can answer. What we do know is that the God of the whole earth desires everyone's salvation. This alone is motivation enough for the church's urgent commitment to Christian mission and evangelism. At the same time, we may hope that Christ, working differently in different circumstances, sometimes utilizes various features of other faiths to draw toward him those who lack sufficient accurate knowledge of him.

3.

In what ways does the Christian church stand in need of repentance for its witness in the world, historically and/or globally?

13

Living in Christ

Key Concepts:
- What are the key components of the story of redemption as Paul develops it? How does Christology shape how we understand this story?
- What does it mean to live "between the times"?
- How does the relationship beween Christology and discipleship come into focus in the expression "in Christ"?
- How do our practices of baptism usher reflection on the person and work of Christ into the midst of the church's life?
- What three dimensions of Christological reflection are inherent to our sharing in the Lord's Supper?

For good reason, the Book of Acts refers to the Christian church and its faith as "the Way." For good reason, Paul conceives of the Christian life as "walking in Christ." Both images belong to the larger metaphor field of **the journey**—in this case, the journey of discipleship. In the end, Christology is about discipleship. That is, knowing the truth about Jesus and knowing Jesus as the truth come through following in his footsteps. These truths are revealed and encountered "on the road."

How might Christology shape faithful life before God? This question has surfaced from time to time in previous chapters. It now remains to explore this question more explicitly. First, I will draw attention to how the advent of Christ locates us within the story of salvation. Second, we will examine the notion of "participation in Christ," so fundamental to Paul's message. Finally, we will look briefly at baptism and at the Lord's Supper as ways in which Christology comes onto center stage in our lives as the church.

Living Between the Times

How decisive for Paul the cross of Christ was for Christian faith and life is perhaps nowhere better seen than in his understanding of the grand story of salvation. Paul sees the past, present, and future in light of that momentous event. Although the Resurrection has inaugurated the new order and is the basis of Christian hope, the period between "first fruits" (Jesus' resurrection) and full harvest (the general resurrection) is marked fundamentally by the cross of Christ. This is why Paul could assert that, while among the Corinthians, he had "decided to know nothing . . . except Jesus Christ, and him crucified" (1 Corinthians 2:2).

How does Paul plot the story of salvation so as to bring to the foreground the immediate relevance and determinative influence of the crucifixion of Jesus Christ? According to Paul's letters, the story of redemption has a number of key components. These include the following:

- the creation of the world and of humanity;
- the transgression of Adam, which marks the invasion of sin and death;
- the communication of God's purpose in covenant with Abraham;
- the election of Israel and the revelation of the law;
- God's sending his Son, Jesus Christ, to redeem humanity and to usher in the new epoch;
- the achievement of God's purpose in the death and resurrection of Jesus;
- the life of the church in the present—cruciform, hopeful, Spirit empowered, mission oriented;
- the final transformation, the new creation, marked by Jesus' return.

Each of these elements of the story is important in its own right; what is crucial for Paul is that we understand where we belong, where our present situation locates us on "the map."

The Thessalonians, for example, had upset the temporal logic of the story as Paul understood it and so misconstrued their present vocation. In 1 Thessalonians 4:13–5:11, Paul indicates his awareness that some were concerned about Christians who had died before the return of Jesus. What will their status be in the end time? Paul addresses this concern with a reminder that the time of Jesus' second coming is still future. Concern with "the times and the seasons" ought to give way to seriousness of purpose and faithfulness rooted in the recollection that Jesus' death "for us" has made possible ongoing life "with him." With reference to Jesus' death, Paul urges his audience to embrace the hope of salvation that differentiates them from the rest of humanity, together with behaviors appropriate to those called to a life determined by the cross (see 1 Thessalonians 1:6; 3:1-5).

A similar situation had developed among the Corinthians. Paul repeatedly attempted to situate the Corinthian believers temporally back at the proper place in the ongoing story of redemption. Particularly in First Corinthians, Paul reflects on the meaning of the crucified Christ in large part so as to counter competing ideas. The word of the cross opposes wrong-headed thinking about the nature of present existence, as though this were the time for triumphalism following the consummation of the new era. Apparently, Paul must remind the Corinthians that the Lord has not yet returned and that the present is reserved for proclaiming the Lord's death "until he comes" (1 Corinthians 11:26). Thus, Paul posits the scandalous cross of Christ as the "power of God" "to us who are being saved." Paul emphasizes "what is weak in the world," "what is low and despised in the world"—that is, "Christ crucified" and the community oriented around the crucified Christ (1 Corinthians 1:18-31).

The Thessalonians and Corinthians had gotten ahead of the story, so to speak. A different problem appeared among the Galatians. From the beginning of his letter to the Galatians, Paul expresses shock that these believers have abandoned the gospel of Jesus Christ in favor of "a different gospel" (1:6). Having regressed to a former moment in the continuing story, they had begun to be persuaded of the importance of circumcision—the hallmark of Jewish identity appropriate to an earlier period. Paul, on the other hand, insists on the centrality of the cross of Christ. Notice how, in Galatians 6:12-17 (author's translation below), he places these two side-by-side in order to contrast two points of time in the grand story of redemption:

Circumcision	*Cross*
It is those who want to make a fair showing in the flesh that are trying to compel you to be circumcised,	
	but only that they might not be persecuted for the cross of Christ.
Even the circumcised do not themselves keep the law, but want you to be circumcised in order that they might boast in your flesh.	
	May I never boast of anything except the cross of our Lord Jesus Christ, through whom the whole world has been crucified to me and I to the world. For neither circumcision nor uncircumcision counts for anything; what counts is new creation.

Circumcision   *Cross*

And as many as will follow this rule,
peace be on them and mercy, as
also on the Israel of God. From now
on let no one cause me trouble,

> for I bear the marks
> of Jesus on my body.

For Paul, the distinction between the circumcised and the uncircumcised, so crucial in former times, has been made irrelevant for the present and future by Jesus' crucifixion.

Paul's churches are not alone in their occasional misconstrual of "the times." Christians today exercise their own tendencies in this respect. We have our own predispositions to disregard the centrality of the cross of Christ for present life. This happens sometimes when we fail to appropriate for ourselves the grace of God present in the cross, so that our lives are marked by guilt and unforgiveness. It happens as well when we fixate on the return of Christ, whether this results in our living in fear of the coming judgment or in triumphalist speculation. And it happens when we assume that our present lives are shaped decisively by the Resurrection, with the result that we have no need to consider how our lives might best reflect the selflessness and devotion to God's aim on display in Jesus' death. We live "between the times," a period that takes its primary orientation from the nature of Jesus' own servitude and self-giving.

Participation in Christ

The centrality for Paul of the concept of living in Christ is measured by the sheer number of its appearances in his letters. Paul uses the expression "in Christ" or "in the Lord" well over one hundred times, often in key passages that clarify for us both the nature of Jesus' person and work and the implications of Paul's Christology for Christian life. More often than not, he uses this language in ways that portray Christian existence as participation in Christ. What does this mean?

First, Paul uses the expression "in Christ" with reference to the saving work of Christ, which is appropriated for the believer. In this case "in Christ" functions as a kind of label, roughly synonymous with the word *Christian*. People who are "in Christ" are understood to have shared in the experiences of Christ, and especially in his death and resurrection (see Romans 6:1-11). People who are "in Christ" are those who have embraced for themselves the saving work of Jesus.

Second, "in Christ" language is sometimes paralleled with "Christ in" language, where it has to do with the presence of Christ in the inner lives of believers. He indwells the lives of believers as a guarantee of everlasting life and as a living resource for faithful living in the present. In this way Christians share fellowship with him, as well as find in this fellowship a source of power against evil and for good.

The notion of fellowship with Christ as a living resource is closely matched in Paul with his description of the benefits of the presence of the Spirit. The Spirit thus serves as the presence of Christ in the believer. In this sense, Paul apparently regarded the Christian life as the continual experience of Christ in the context of all of one's being and doing, as a constant companion.

To be "in Christ" is also to live in submission to his lordship. Just as Jesus' faithfulness to God has become effective for our salvation, so our salvation is demonstrated in our faithfulness to him. Our "walk in Christ" is a life in his footsteps, in obedience to him.

This does not mean that life "in Christ" is a subjective mode of existence for individuals. Being "in Christ" locates one necessarily within the community of others who are "in Christ." This is the body of Christ, whose members belong to one another and whose chief points of identity are the work of Christ on their behalf and the life of Christ which serves as their model.

Finally, being "in Christ" has to do with the new perspective we have in Christ. As Paul spells it out in 2 Corinthians 5, those who are "in Christ" have crossed the threshold of revelation, have donned a new lens by which to perceive the world, and therefore participate in God's "new creation." It is not simply that the believer is in the

1,

As you reflect on the character of your life "in Christ," to what degree would you say that being "in Christ" has located you within the community of believers?

process of being transformed into greater Christlikeness; rather, it is that she or he perceives the cosmos differently. Enmity has been replaced with friendship, so that the existence of believers is no longer worked out from the standpoint of estrangement with God, nor with the human family, nor with the world of nature. Harmony and coherence are possible in a way that had not been the case. Divisions—whether based on race or ethnicity or nationality or gender or social status—are baseless and therefore no longer serve as categories of meaningful interaction.

Two Focal Points of "Lived Christology"

Christology, our understanding of Jesus' person and work, is mediated to us in many forms and through various media. Chief among these may indeed be the songs and hymns of our worship, though the liturgical affirmations of our common faith (such as in the Apostles' Creed) may also have a central role, along with sermons and study groups. Since earliest Christian times, two constants in the lives of Jesus' followers have helped to focus our reflection on Christ and his work: baptism and the Lord's Supper. Both were practiced among the earliest churches and undoubtedly helped to generate firmer understandings of Jesus' person and work.

Baptism

Within the pages of the New Testament, the subject of baptism comes up with regularity. Two perspectives are especially relevant to our interest in Christology, however: the Acts of the Apostles and Paul.

In the narrative of Acts, Luke does not so much sketch out a theology of baptism as demonstrate one. It is true that in Acts 2:38, we read of Peter's setting forth a kind of model response to the Christian message. His audience interrupted his sermon at Pentecost, inquiring, "Brothers, what should we do?" (Acts 2:37). Peter replied, "Repent, and be baptized every one of you in the name of Jesus Christ so that your sins may be forgiven; and you will receive the gift of the Holy Spirit." Evidently, then, baptism "in the name of

Jesus" is a normal, expected response. Within the two volumes of the Lukan narrative, baptism takes its meaning in part from the ministry of John (Luke 3:1-20), with the result that it expresses a desire to embrace God's purpose anew and to be embraced into the community of those similarly oriented around the way of God. That is, baptism is both "response" and "gift." New believers signal through their willingness to be baptized that they have embraced the good news and desire a life lived in the service of the kingdom of God. In baptizing new believers, the community of faith demonstrates its belief that these persons have received divine forgiveness and thus visibly incorporates them into the family of God's people. From the one side, then, baptism is a response to the divine offer of salvation, while from the other it is one of the blessings of salvation.

Additionally, baptism, according to the Pentecost address of Peter in Acts 2, is "in the name of Jesus Christ" (Acts 2:38). In this way "the name" provides an integrating focus for this community, a focus that is dependent on one's embracing the new way of construing God's purpose articulated by Peter in Acts 2:14-36. In particular, it means that persons consent to Peter's argument that the "Lord" on whose name people are to call for salvation according to Joel 2:28-32 (see Acts 2:21) is none other than Jesus of Nazareth. That is, it requires one to acknowledge Jesus' status as Lord and Christ, God's coregent, and, if this, then to incarnate the attitudes, commitments, and behaviors characteristic of discipleship as this is represented in Jesus' ministry and spelled out in Jesus' teachings.

John the Baptist had already made a similar point. As this is represented in Luke 3, John had proclaimed that authentic repentance would become visible in the lives of the repentant. Their lives would bear "fruits worthy of repentance" (Luke 3:8), especially as this is represented in material care for the needy, business practices that do not exploit, and the like (Luke 3:10-14). Baptism "in the name of Jesus" raises the stakes even further, for it invites contemplation on the whole of the narrative of Jesus' life and, thus, on the whole of his teaching on the character of discipleship. God himself affirmed this in Jesus' resurrection and ascension. Following God means following God *in this way,* that is, in the way set forth by Jesus of Nazareth.

Baptism in the narrative of Acts, then, is essentially centered on Christ and is a prominent, visible means by which persons are incorporated into the community of God's people whose lives are centered on following Christ.

The significance of baptism to Paul is suggested already by the symbolism he often employs: "As many of you as were baptized into Christ have clothed yourselves with Christ" (Galatians 3:27). The imagery of stripping off clothes and putting on clean ones is well-known (for example, Isaiah 52:1; 61:10; Zechariah 3:1-5) and connotes the character of baptism as a transformation of life. Those being baptized "took off" their old lives and "put on" Christ. This act associates one intimately with the family of God's people (whose status as God's children is thus marked by baptism and not through tracing their genealogy to Abraham) and brings one into union with Christ. Baptism, therefore, is an important rite of passage; and it signals one's participation with Christ.

In Romans 6:1-11, the union with Christ signified in baptism is spelled out in terms of the appropriation of the blessings of salvation through baptism. This passage is not concerned with the "mode" of baptism (immersion? sprinkling? pouring?) but with its meaning. Accordingly, those who are baptized are said by Paul to have joined Christ in his death and resurrection. They are "baptized into his death" (6:3) and are therefore "dead to sin" (6:11); that is, sin has no more reign over them. Jesus' death, Paul insists, is representative of our own, with the result that we also share in his resurrection life (compare Colossians 2:11-12). We are freed from the domination of sin in our lives so that we might live for him who died and was raised for us (2 Corinthians 5:14-15). We may walk in "newness of life" (Romans 6:4). Jesus, we noted in Chapter 4, inaugurated a new humanity. In Romans 6, baptism portrays the death of the old humanity, which is then replaced by the new. The old order has passed, and the new is at work as Christians in baptism appropriate for themselves the saving work of Christ and submit to Christ as Lord.

2.

Think about the way your church celebrates baptism and the Lord's Supper. Are there ways in which the importance of the whole church for Christian discipleship might be made even plainer in these moments of celebration?

In at least three ways, then, baptism ushers Christological reflection directly into the lived experience of the church. Baptism calls forth from us reflection on the nature of the work of Christ, whose death and resurrection are representative of our own. Baptism calls forth from us a firm declaration of allegiance to Jesus as Lord. And baptism initiates us into a life of discipleship in which our lives are transformed into the new humanity set forth in Jesus' own ministry.

The Lord's Supper

Christology in all its expressions comes most centrally into focus for the community of Christ in the Lord's Supper (also known as Communion or the Eucharist). Here we celebrate the ongoing significance of Jesus' life for us and, indeed, for the whole world. Here we are met by the risen Lord himself. And here we proclaim the death of Christ until he comes. Here reside the three dimensions of Christological reflection.

There is first the *retrospective* dimension. As we celebrate the Lord's Supper, we recall the mighty acts of deliverance that characterize God's activity on behalf of his people and affirm together that his ultimate act of salvation took the form of the death of Jesus, God's Son. This was not God's decision for Jesus, rendering Jesus as nothing more than the hapless victim in a cosmic drama. As Paul affirms, "God proves his love for us in that while we still were sinners Christ died for us" (Romans 5:8). The cross is the outworking of God's will, to be sure; but it is at the same time the outworking of Christ's own choice. Here, in Jesus' death, we find the utmost expression of a life lived for others. Our life in Christ thus has deep roots in the past, and in Communion we embrace that past as definitive for the character of our own lives.

In the Lord's Supper we find on display, secondly, the *prospective* dimension of Christology. After citing the ancient tradition of the church regarding Jesus' last meal with his disciples, Paul notes, "As often as you eat this bread and drink the cup, you proclaim the Lord's death until he comes" (1 Corinthians 11:26). The Lord's Supper thus anticipates the future that God has willed, a future that is depicted throughout Scripture as a heavenly banquet where even the most unlikely of people are hosted by God, where the hungry are never without food, and where all bask in the fellowship of Jesus Christ. In the eucharistic meal we express our longing for God's will to be done fully on earth as it is in heaven and our confidence that the fullness of Christ's vision of God's purpose will be realized. Our hope as Christians thus comes into clearest focus in Communion.

Finally, the Lord's Supper presents also the *reflexive* dimension of Christology. That is, in the celebration of Christ's work on our behalf, we are invited to reflect back on our own lives. We experience the Lord's Table as a mirror, reminding us of our deepest commitments and calling us forward to a life in which those convictions are fully realized.

"Do this in remembrance of me" is a request not only to partake of the bread and the cup as symbols of the love of God but also "to remember." The pattern of this remembering reads like a litany in the Old Testament: "Then God remembered . . . and acted." Memory in this case is no mere cognitive exercise but an impetus to act. Similarly, "proclaiming the Lord's death" is not mentioned by Paul as a job description for preachers only but for all who participate in the Supper. This is because "proclaiming" and "remembering" in this case interpret each other. At the Eucharist, we remember the selfless love of Christ (whose commitment to God and thus to the needy outstripped any human instincts for self-preservation and self-aggrandizement); we evaluate the shape of our own lives as we stand in the shadow of the cross of Christ; and we commit ourselves to proclaim in our own lives, in our words and deeds, the character of his service on humanity's behalf.

In these and other lived moments of the body of Christ, we come face to face with the significance of Jesus for us. We remember the shape of his life, the substance of his message, and the nature of his death, all of which have meaning for our understanding of his identity and work and for the character of our own discipleship. It is under

3.

With regard to your participation in this sustained exploration of BEGINNING WITH JESUS, how have you been challenged in your understanding of Christ and your experience of discipleship? What responses seem appropriate in light of those challenges?

the sign of the cross and in hope of the resurrection that we come to him and that we are being saved through our union with Christ. We follow in his footsteps, denying ourselves and taking up the cross, and find ourselves being transformed by the Spirit of Christ into the likeness of Christ. Under his lordship, our attitudes and commitments and practices take on the nature of holy love, so that our relationships are redeemed as well. And we discover that the work of Christ is not only for us, but for all, and not only for the human family, but for all that God has created. Jesus is Lord of all.